Helen Balkwill Harris, James Rendel Harris

Letters From the Scenes of the Recent Massacres in Armenia

Helen Balkwill Harris, James Rendel Harris

Letters From the Scenes of the Recent Massacres in Armenia

ISBN/EAN: 9783744717496

Printed in Europe, USA, Canada, Australia, Japan

Cover: Foto ©ninafisch / pixelio.de

More available books at **www.hansebooks.com**

LETTERS FROM ARMENIA

Introductory Letter from Mr. Gladstone.

*Hawarden Castle,
Chester,
Jan. 14, 1897.*

Dear Mr. Rendel Harris,

I am very glad to hear that you intend to publish a volume of your letters on your experiences while distributing relief and travelling through Armenia.

I am sure that it is of great importance that all the information possible should be given on this subject, especially where it can be given at first hand.

Yours faithfully,

W. E. GLADSTONE.

LETTERS

FROM THE SCENES OF THE
RECENT MASSACRES IN

ARMENIA

BY

J. RENDEL HARRIS

AND

HELEN B. HARRIS

London
JAMES NISBET & CO., LIMITED
21 BERNERS STREET
1897

PREFACE

THE following letters consist of a correspondence carried on by my wife and myself with a small circle of interested friends in England who followed our expedition to Armenia in the spring of the present year with every form of sympathy, spiritual, moral, and material. As often happens in such cases, the information which we were able to send concerning the condition of affairs in the interior of Asiatic Turkey was soon in demand by others than those for whom it was initially designed; and when the channels which we had marked for our little stream of testimony had once been overflowed, it was not easy to refuse the request of a leading London firm of publishers who wished to make our brook into a river (with appropriate banks of copyright). And so, though we had no intention in the first instance of allowing general publicity to these letters, we have in the end agreed that they may be reproduced.

One reason, which encourages us to believe that they may be further helpful in the cause of the redemption of the Eastern Christians from Turkish tyranny, lies in the fact that they have already been the means of convincing some thoughtful persons of the gravity of the issues involved. And this has been accomplished, as I suppose, not by any extravagant tale of horrors, nor by the recapitulation of stories of unnatural cruelty and crime, but by the rude sketch which the letters furnish of the Armenian national life and character as seen by those who have taken time for the study, and who are both sympathetic and critical in their attitude towards these unfortunate people, so as not to underrate their virtues, nor, on the other hand, to be blind to their faults. We were soon compelled to recognise that civilisation in Armenia was making very rapid strides indeed, even in face of a tyranny which had assiduously encompassed the destruction of "the whole forest of civility," as Wordsworth calls it, and which in recent repressive measures had "doomed it to perish, to the last fair tree." But of a genuine civilisation it may be said, as of a truly progressive religion (and the Armenians have both), that the forces which are with us are more than those that are against us.

The moderate tone of the letters was necessary, too, in a country where correspondence was continually in danger of being intercepted by the authorities; but it must not be assumed that we have told more than a fraction of the misery which we have seen, or reported more than a very small fraction of the horrors of which we have heard.

Some trifling expansions have been made by means of footnotes for the sake of persons who may not have followed the story of Armenian undoing so closely as to be familiar with all the historical matters alluded to.

PREFACE

I take this opportunity of thanking those friends who have helped us hitherto in the prosecution of our journey and in the circulation of the letters, especially Mr. F. W. Crossley of Manchester, whose advice and assistance have been invaluable to us. Dr. R. Hingston Fox, who took upon himself the burden of the transcription and distribution of our bulletins, and our friend Edmund Wright Brooks, who acted and still acts as treasurer of the fund which the Society of Friends opened on our account, and whose sympathetic co-operation has been given to us so freely through the whole of this difficult expedition.

J. RENDEL HARRIS.

CONTENTS

LETTER	PAGE
I. ARRIVAL AT CONSTANTINOPLE—VISIT TO THE BRITISH EMBASSY	1
II. VISIT TO JUDGE TARRING—A FRIENDS' MEETING IN STAMBOUL—ROBERT COLLEGE—VISIT TO THE PATRIARCH IZMIRLIAN—FRIENDS OF THE SUFFERING ARMENIANS AT CHALCEDON, ETC.	6
III. ARRIVAL OF THE "TESKEREH"—THE NEWLY DISCOVERED SIXTH-CENTURY GOSPELS	15
IV. PROJECTED DEPARTURE FROM SMYRNA TO ALEXANDRETTA—AN AMERICAN LADY MISSIONARY FROM THE INTERIOR—POSSIBILITY OF ARMENIAN EMIGRATION	17
V. ARRIVAL AT ALEXANDRETTA—START FOR THE INTERIOR	22
VI. JOURNEY TO AINTAB—TROUBLES AT KILLIS—AN EARLY START BAULKED—A HARD NIGHT—ARRIVAL AT AINTAB	27
VII. AMERICAN BRAVERY—OFFICIAL HYPOCRISY AND FATALISM—DETAILS OF THE GREAT MASSACRE—INSULTS TO ENGLAND—OCCUPATIONS OF ARMENIAN WOMEN—SOME COMPASSIONATE TURKS, ETC.	30
VIII. AMERICAN CIVILISATION IN THE MIDST OF TURKISH DESOLATION—REVIVAL OF RELIGION IN AINTAB—REMARKABLE SERVICES IN THE OLD GREGORIAN AND PROTESTANT CHURCHES	41
IX. CROSSING THE EUPHRATES—DRYING UP OF THE GREAT RIVER—DIFFUSION OF THE KURDS—MISS SHATTUCK, THE HEROINE OF OURFA, ETC.	49
X. A MORNING WITH MISS SHATTUCK AT OURFA	54
XI. HOUSE HIRED IN OURFA—ANCIENT LEGENDS OF EDESSA—RELIEF WORK IN THE CITY—AN ARCHÆOLOGICAL PUZZLE, ETC.	59
XII. VISIT TO THE BURNED CHURCH—A CALL UPON THE PASHA'S WIFE—HER WARM SYMPATHY WITH THE SUFFERING PEOPLE, ETC.	68

CONTENTS

LETTER		PAGE
XIII.	A COMMUNICATION FROM SOME LEADING EDESSANS	75
XIV.	SCHEMES OF RELIEF AND SOCIAL RECONSTRUCTION—ORPHANS, WIDOWS, AND SCHOOLS	81
XV.	OUR FOURTH SUNDAY IN OURFA—WOMEN'S MEETING IN THE PROTESTANT CHURCH—AN ARMENIAN BETROTHAL—LETTERS FROM MISSIONARIES	88
XVI.	WE LEAVE OURFA AND VISIT GARMOUSH AND SEVEREK—A NIGHT IN A HOVEL—MASSACRE IN SEVEREK—OUR SERVANT CLAPPED IN PRISON—A NIGHT IN A KURDISH TENT—ARRIVAL AT DIARBEKIR	96
XVII.	DIFFICULTIES AT DIARBEKIR—A ROUGH RIDE TO MARDIN—EXCURSION IN SEARCH OF MSS.—ALEXANDER IN TROUBLE AGAIN	103
XVIII.	CLOSING OF THE HIGH SCHOOL—IMPOSING CEREMONIES—VISIT TO THE JACOBITE SCHOOLS, ETC.	109
XIX.	FIRST RUMOURS OF THE VAN MASSACRE	113
XX.	A MODERN SIMEON STYLITES—BRIEF ACCOUNT OF A VISIT TO THE TÛR ABDÎN—VISIT TO A TURKISH PRISON, ETC.	115
XXI.	JOURNEY FROM MARDIN TO DIARBEKIR—FORDING THE TIGRIS RIVER—INCIDENT AT A DESOLATED VILLAGE—NATURE AND EFFECTS OF THE MASSACRE AT DIARBEKIR—THE FRENCH CONSUL—PLANS FOR FUTURE MOVEMENTS	123
XXII.	ATTEMPTS AT RELIEF IN DIARBEKIR AND NEIGHBOURHOOD—A REVIEW OF HAMIDIYEH CAVALRY, ETC.—A SAD LETTER FROM AINTAB	130
XXIII.	JOURNEY FROM DIARBEKIR TO HARPOOT—TAURUS MOUNTAINS—SOURCE OF THE TIGRIS—HEROIC BAND OF MISSIONARIES AT HARPOOT: STORY OF THEIR PRESERVATION DURING THE MASSACRE AND IN THE PRESENCE OF DEATH	141
XXIV.	HOW TO HELP THE DESOLATED VILLAGES?—CONDITION AROUND HARPOOT—DESPAIR OF THE VILLAGERS—PETITION FROM HOO-I-LOO FOR REBUILDING OF PROTESTANT CHURCH—VISIT TO THE VILLAGE IN RUINS—MEAL IN AN ORCHARD—ASSESSING THE TAXES OF THE DEAD UPON THE SURVIVORS—PLANS FOR FUTURE WORK—VAN, MALATIA, ETC.	147

CONTENTS

LETTER

XXV. VIGOROUS PROTESTS AGAINST WESTERN SCEPTICISM—DIFFICULTIES OF RELIEF WORK—REBUILDING OF VILLAGES, ETC. 155

XXVI. DETENTION AT HARPOOT OWING TO DIFFICULTIES OF TRANSIT—STORY OF A YOUNG ARMENIAN, JUST RECOVERED FROM HIS WOUNDS, NOW PUT IN PRISON—QUESTION OF THE RELEASE OF THE MANY IMPRISONED ARMENIANS; IS BRIBERY LAWFUL?—A HARD CASE—EXAMPLE OF THE EARLY CHURCH—THE MISSIONARIES' DECISION—LETTER FROM OURFA—TEACHING THE WOMEN AND GIRLS—WORK FOR THE ORPHANS—"HARRIS HOME" IN FULL OPERATION—ONLY THOSE ENTIRELY ORPHANED CAN BE HELPED . 160

XXVII. ARRIVAL AT MALATIA—EXTENSIVE DISTRESS THERE—A PARADISE CITY—ACCOUNT OF THE MASSACRE—THE RUINS TO-DAY—HOW TO HELP THE PEOPLE—THE REFORM COMMISSIONER—LARGE MEETING IN A GARDEN—DEPARTURE OF J. R. H.—PASSPORTS FOR THE TWO SERVANTS—INTERVIEW WITH SHAKIR PASHA, AND WITH THE PASHA'S WIFE IN THE HAREM—A FRIENDLY BEY WHO HELPED THE ARMENIANS—EMBROIDERY WORK—BOARDING OUT THE ORPHANS; FIVE POUNDS FOR ONE YEAR—THE PRESS OF TEARFUL WOMEN—CONFISCATING THE FRUIT IN THE GARDENS—PERSECUTION OF KURDS WHO REFUSED TO MASSACRE—MISS BUSH AND DR. GATES . . . 166

XXVIII. OUR LAST DAY IN MALATIA; A BUSY CROWD—SELECTING FIFTY ORPHANS OUT OF FIFTEEN HUNDRED—DEPARTURE—GOODNESS OF SOME MOSLEMS—THE ZAPTIEHS—JOURNEY BACK TO HARPOOT BEGUILED BY HYMNS—WELCOME AT HARPOOT—PLANS FOR VAN 175

MEMORANDUM: NOTES OF INFORMATION FROM J. R. H. . 180

XXIX. PRIVATE LETTER OF THANKS FOR UNEXPECTED CONTRIBUTION—BUILDING OF SCHOOLS, ETC., AT MALATIA—THE PEOPLE SET CHURCH BEFORE HOUSES—ONE THOUSAND CHILDREN TO BE ACCOMMODATED—A JOINT SCHOOL BOARD—UNION OF THE CHURCHES 191

XXX. JOURNEY TO VAN PUT ASIDE FOR THE PRESENT—HEMMED IN AT HARPOOT—SIGNS OF TROUBLE AROUND—PRESENCE OF H. B. H. "A SAFEGUARD TO THE TOWN"—COLLEGE FLOURISHING—H. B. H. ILL WITH MALARIAL FEVER—THE GREAT NEED OF HELP FOR THE ORPHANS . . 199

LETTER		PAGE
XXXI.	SUMMARY BY R. H. F. OF PRIVATE LETTER FROM H. B. H—SYMPTOMS OF FURTHER MASSACRES—THE BLOW FELL AT EGHIN—HARPOOT THREATENED—STATE OF TERROR—THE PROTESTANTS TO BE SUPPRESSED—REPORT OF THE EGHIN MASSACRE	206
XXXII.	INTENDED VISIT TO EGHIN — FURTHER REPORT OF THE MASSACRE THERE — TWO LETTERS FROM PROTESTANT ARMENIANS IN NEIGHBOURING TOWNS	212
XXXIII.	LETTER FROM J. R. H., NARRATING HIS JOURNEY OUT OF ARMENIA IN AUGUST, VISITING KHANGAL, SIVAS: MARTYRDOM OF PASTOR—TOKAT: TOMB OF HENRY MARTYN—MARSOVAN—AMASIA; CLIMATE OF PONTUS; TERTULLIAN ON MARCION—SAMSOUN—REPORT ON REBUILDING VILLAGES—FURTHER REPORT ON EGHIN MASSACRE	217
XXXIV.	ON THE EVE OF SETTING OUT FROM HARPOOT FOR ARABKIR AND EGHIN—THE LATE PANIC; MASSACRE AVERTED—THAT AT EGHIN CARRIED OUT BY THE CITIZENS; ALLEGED REVOLUTIONARY CAUSE FALSE—AT ARABKIR, THE PEOPLE STARVING—THE REPAIRED SCHOOLHOUSE AT HARPOOT WELL FILLED—COLLEGE DOING EXCELLENT WORK	227
XXXV.	DEPARTURE FROM HARPOOT—DELAYS, FAREWELLS—TOILSOME JOURNEY—ARABKIR—A FINE CITY, IN RUINS—THE BETTER CLASSES IN POVERTY—VISITS FROM THE WOMEN TILL STOPPED BY THE GOVERNOR—A HEROIC TURKISH ZAPTIEH; VISIT TO HIS SICK-BED	231
XXXVI.	LETTER FROM H. B. H.—VISITING THE WOMEN AT ARABKIR; A MEETING WITH THEM—DISORDER HARSHLY QUELLED BY THE SEXTON—JOURNEY TO EGHIN: A ROMANTIC LITTLE CITY, RUINS OF BEAUTIFUL HOUSES; SAD TALES OF THE MASSACRE THERE, AND AT FIVE NEAR VILLAGES—THE BEREAVED WOMEN IN THEIR HOMES — PROVISION OF WHEAT, BEDDING, ETC., FOR WINTER NEEDS — LETTER FROM MISS BUSH, EGHIN—LETTER FROM MISS SHATTUCK, OURFA	238
XXXVII.	JOURNEY FROM SIVAS TO MARSOVAN VIA TOKAT—HARD TRAVEL—WELCOME AT MARSOVAN—AN IDEAL MISSION THERE—TOILSOME JOURNEY TO SAMSOUN—LETTER FROM HARPOOT, STATING PRESENT DIFFICULTIES AND THE APPARENT INTENTION OF THE GOVERNMENT TO CLOSE THE MISSION SCHOOLS, ETC.—RELIEF WORK IN EGHIN	249

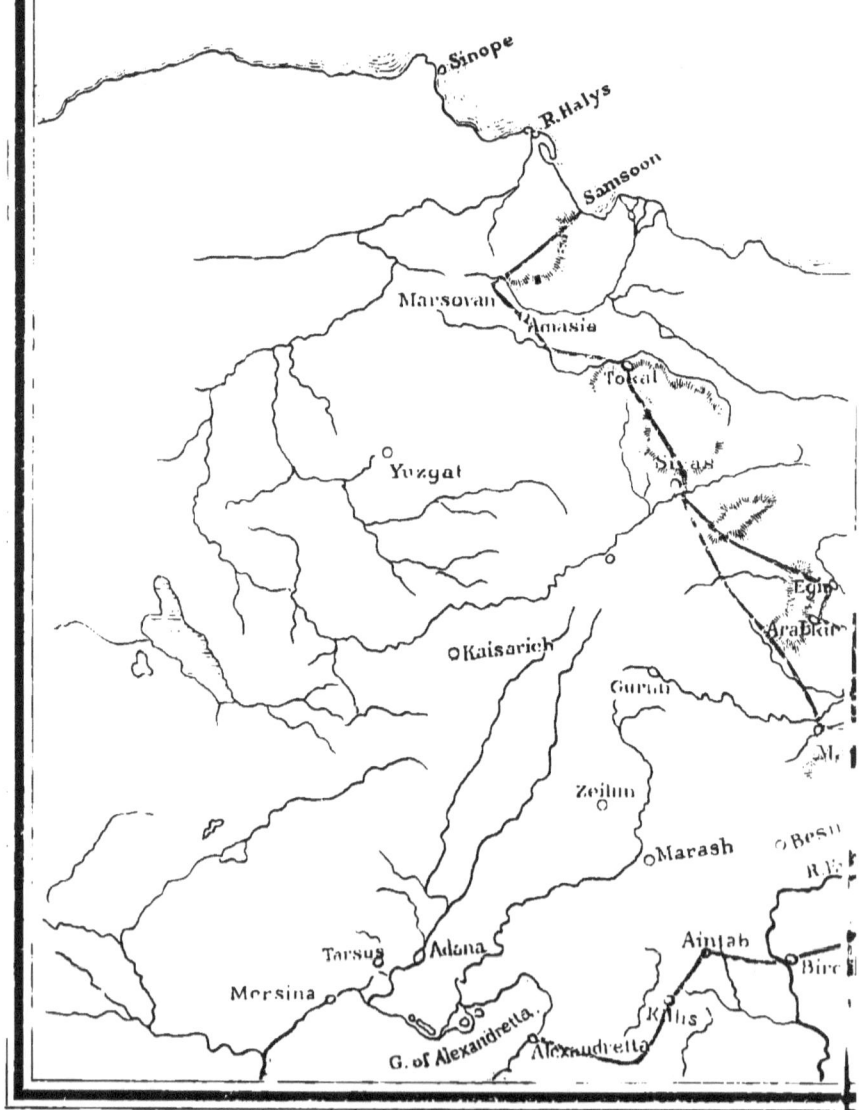

LETTERS FROM ARMENIA

LETTER No. I.

ARRIVAL AT CONSTANTINOPLE—VISIT TO THE
BRITISH EMBASSY.

CONSTANTINOPLE, *March* 28, 1896.

DEAR FRIENDS,—We arrived here safely, as we expected, on the afternoon of March 25, the weather being gloriously fine, though much cooler than in Paris, and after some Custom House difficulty drove through the crowded streets to the Hotel in Pera, where for several days we have been most comfortably housed, though now we have removed to the house of our most kind and hospitable friends, G. D. and his wife, where we feel quite settled and at home.

R. sent his letter of introduction from Mr. Atkin, with our cards, to the British Embassy immediately on our arrival, and in the evening of the same day, kindly accompanied by Mrs. D., we called on Clara Barton,[1] and heard

[1] President of the American Red Cross Society.

from her and Mr. Pullman a most interesting account of their experience since coming here. She said that they had been very kindly treated by the Turkish Minister for Foreign Affairs, and that the English newspapers were wrong in saying that every obstacle had been placed in their way. Four gentlemen, agents of the Red Cross, are now *en route* for Armenia, by way of Smyrna, viz., Dr. Hubbell and Mr. Mason; and Messrs. Wistar and Wood, who left by the last steamer for Alexandretta. Large supplies of clothing have gone with them, and sewing-machines as well! These have all gone with a simple Turkish passport, not waiting for the Iradè, which is still in cloudland.

We feel much sympathy for Miss Barton and party, however, in the fact that Mrs. Mason, the only other lady who came with them, and mother of one of the two gentlemen who went off first, died on the day of our arrival from bronchitis, &c., no doubt intensified by travel and the change of climate. She was buried the next day, and her loss will leave Miss Barton, who will not herself attempt to travel further, very lonely.

On Thursday morning we called at the British Embassy, but were asked to come again in the afternoon. Later we received an informal note from one of the attachés, enclosing two invitations from Sir Philip and Lady Currie, one for an afternoon reception the same day at five, and the other for dinner *en petit comité* for yesterday. This we took as very encouraging, and then went with

Mrs. D. to a bazaar got up in aid of the Armenians. Here we met some of the most interesting English residents in Constantinople, and had several nice talks, and heard many things which cannot be put on paper. Evidently the feeling here is a very deep-seated one; but spies abound, and you have the consciousness all the time that you have to be very careful when you speak at all freely.

Duly at five we were at the Embassy, and were ushered from staircase to staircase, and from one grand salon to another, till at last we came to the Reception Rooms, and met our ambassador and his lovely wife. They were both most cordial; but the room was fast filling with visitors, and beyond a few friendly sympathetic words we did not get any private conversation. People here say that either the Sultan is entirely controlled by some Palace clique, or that he is the "most remarkable man," because all the massacres *have certainly been ordered from the Palace*, and yet he will at times express the most humane sympathies. We heard that our Embassy is in great ill-favour, and any Turk of consequence who ventures to come there is at once a marked man.

Yesterday morning R. and I thought we would take the opportunity of a quiet time and go to see St. Sophia. Previously we had been asked at the Embassy if we would go to the Selamlik, but we declined, saying we knew the Sultan's portrait *quite well*. Yesterday, however, was extra grand, because Prince Ferdinand was to be received by the Sultan, and all the world attended;

and a gentleman told me afterwards the Sultan was treated as if he were a god!

On our way to St. Sophia and on the Galata Bridge we met all the Turkish cavalry, lancers, &c.; and R. pointed out that their dress was in most respects just as in the time of the Crusaders and earlier, and that the musical instruments of the mounted band were far earlier and even Biblical in character.[1]

St. Sophia has been so often described that I will not add mine to other accounts, but simply say that it impressed me more than St. Peter's, and less than the Mosque of Omar.

In the evening we went to the Embassy, and Sir Philip told R. that he would do all in his power to help us, and thought we should be able to get to the places we want, particularly to Diarbekir.

This afternoon we are going up the Bosphorus to stay the night at the country-house of the British Consular Judge, Mr. Tarring — who has also promised to help us all he can—and other invitations are coming in.

I might add before closing this long letter, that this morning Mrs. D. and I went to an Armenian shop in Stamboul and purchased a quantity of material which we got under cost price, and which poor Armenian women are already set at work to make up into garments for us

---

[1] Alluding, I suppose, to the Parthian kettledrums mounted on horseback, which are described in Apoc. ix. under the figure of the humming of the wings of locusts.—J. R. H.

to carry.[1]—With love, I remain for us both, very affectionately,

HELEN B. H.

[1] As a warning to those who may be engaged in similar philanthropic attempts to get clothes to the backs of people in the interior, it may be as well to confess that this piece of charity did not reach its destination at Harpoot until October, by which time the contents of the boxes were very much "minished and brought low."—J. R. H.

LETTER No. II.

VISIT TO JUDGE TARRING—A FRIENDS' MEETING IN STAMBOUL—
ROBERT COLLEGE—VISIT TO THE PATRIARCH IZMIRLIAN—
FRIENDS OF THE SUFFERING ARMENIANS AT CHALCEDON, ETC.

CONSTANTINOPLE, *April* 1.

DEAR FRIENDS,—So many things have happened since I last wrote that I hardly know what to tell first, but perhaps a brief journal account is best. In the afternoon of Saturday, March 28, we went up the Bosphorus with Judge Tarring to Bebek, the place of his country residence, and also the landing-stage for Robert College, which is on the height above, in a magnificent situation. The steam up the Bosphorus was most interesting; one palace which we passed was the one in which poor Abdul Aziz, the Sultan's uncle, committed suicide, and the next to it had just been done up to receive Prince Ferdinand. Mr. Tarring said a fortnight ago it was a wretched tumble-down place, but numbers of workmen had been put on, and now it was quite gay. A little further up still was the palace to which the Khedive comes when he visits Constantinople. Bebek is nearly half-way up the Bosphorus, and close by the great towers built by Mohammed II. before taking Constantinople. They are very picturesque now. Close by also is the spot where Darius crossed on his bridge of boats.

A number of English and American friends met us to tea at our friends' hospitable home, principally those connected with the college, and the president and his wife, Dr. and Mrs. Washburn, and Dr. Long and his daughter and others came to dinner. Mrs. Washburn has a sister, a Mrs. Lea, who is a missionary at Marash, and she told us some awful accounts of sufferings. They are feeding thousands there daily, at the rate of $2\frac{1}{2}$d. a week each. This only gives bread, and sickness of various kinds prevails. These ladies told me that they had been hard at work all the winter making garments, that Armenian merchants had given their committee about £1000 worth of material (first and last), and that they themselves had sent over 3000 garments, yet this is nothing to what is needed. At Erzeroum the clothing has been pretty well distributed, but only very imperfectly elsewhere.

On Sunday we came into the city with the Tarrings, and while they went to the *one* evangelical English place of worship in the city, we went to the Friends' meeting and mission, in which we were deeply interested. All present, except the mission staff, ourselves, and one Turk, were Armenians; and both R. and I, in our words to them, which Dr. D. interpreted, dwelt on the present situation, and endeavoured to encourage them with ourselves to an unwavering trust in God through all.

Then came lunch, and then a mission meeting, when we both spoke again, but this time simply to tell the story in few words of the Saviour's love for sinners. We then shook hands with every one present, and some of the dear people were *very loving*. The indefatigable mission party now turned their attention to the Sunday-school, while we left and steamed up the Bosphorus once more, as R. had promised to address the college in the evening.

This audience was a very different one to the morning one. About two hundred students, besides professors and wives and friends, were present, and a very mixed audience; they were ecclesiastically Armenians, Catholics, Greek Church, and Jews, besides Protestants. R. spoke on the direct communication of God to the soul of man by the Spirit, and told some of his own early experience —a thing I never heard him do in public before—but I think it was the right thing for boys like these, who are too much brought up to separate religious doctrine from personal conduct. We slept at Dr. Washburn's house that night, and returned to the city in the morning with Judge Tarring.

That afternoon (Monday) we visited M. Izmirlian, the Armenian Patriarch, and Dr. and Mrs. D. accompanied us, Dr. D. interpreting. We had a card from Dr. Baronian, of Manchester, to introduce us, and the Patriarch said he had also received a letter from him about our visit.

He is a noble old man, but extremely sad-looking—indeed, " sad " is too mild a word, " broken-hearted" would be better. We were quite alone with him in his private room, and the ecclesiastic who brought in coffee immediately retired. He spoke very warmly and gratefully of the efforts of English people, " Friends " and others, to relieve his suffering nation, but with *intense surprise and indignation* at the lack of action on the part of the Christian nations politically. He said that so systematic a persecution, which was *not* a mere wave of fanaticism, was unparalleled in history. Monsters like Nero, he said, have flooded the world with blood, and then disappeared; "*but our suffering has no respite, no end!*" He gave us his blessing as we rose to go, and we also said that we prayed God to keep and sustain and bless him in his most arduous position.

He impressed us greatly, and Lady Currie told me later in the day that she looked upon him as a holy man, or as if he were almost an apostle. The Sultan has not only threatened but tried to buy him by offers of the greatest favours, but he can neither be bribed nor intimidated; and yet, if he thought it would be for his people's good, no personal love of power would for a moment weigh with him to prevent him resigning.[1] They say that an unprincipled Armenian has just been offered £10,000 to bring about his downfall.

After our visit to the Patriarch we went to afternoon tea with Mr. and Mrs. ——, Mr. —— being the correspondent of the *Daily* ——. There we heard much about the condition of the European press, and of the immense number of papers in the Sultan's pay. There is a gentleman in Constantinople (whose name we heard) who has taken an enormous sum to contradict the facts sent to the English papers from the interior by Mr. —— and others. This man is ostracised by all English people here, and so

[1] His resignation has since been forced, and the good Patriarch is in exile at Jerusalem.—J. R. H.

pays some penalty for his Judas-like action. The Sultan, it is said, spends untold sums in bribes, and not less than £40,000 a month in paying spies as well.

After our visit to the ——'s we crossed the Bosphorus, and went to the ancient village of Chalcedon (where an early Church Council, which condemned the Monophysite doctrine, was held A.D. 451), where Mr. and Mrs. Whittall and their family reside in a lovely home commanding a perfectly exquisite view of Constantinople, with St. Sophia rising above the buildings of the Seraglio, and mosques and minarets standing out against the eastern sky in perfectly distinct beauty, while every prosaic detail is too distant to interfere.

Mr. W. is chairman of the Relief Committee in Constantinople, which is mixed in nationality, Americans and English working together under him in perfect harmony. He had just read a budget of letters by the same post from different parts of the interior, which he said he should send on direct to the Duke of Westminster's Committee. I do hope some of the particulars will be published. One hundred thousand people at least are being kept alive now through their efforts. Three thousand pounds has just gone to Ourfa, but the needs are unspeakable. The wicked Turks have cut up the Armenian vineyards by the roots at Marash, &c., and taken all their agricultural implements, as well as all their household utensils, from the people, not leaving a spade or a kettle; and all that is being done now is just to try and keep the absolutely helpless from dying, ordinary poverty not being assisted, and every kind of disease is rife. Camp fever, from lack of food, &c. &c., and from contact with every kind of pollution, is present, and in Marash both missionaries and doctors (two out of four) are themselves down with it. Mr. W. and his wife *urge* us to go there if we *possibly* can; it is I think about eight days from Ourfa.

We left Chalcedon (the modern name of which is Yadi Keui) yesterday morning, after a very stormy night, and drove to Scutari, where the crossing was feasible. Yesterday afternoon I had a very interesting visit with Lady Currie for about an hour.

Mr. Terrill has, you know, returned to America. The Sultan, either before he left or just after, sent orders to Bitlis for the American missionaries to leave, which caused a panic here; but short measures were taken with him by the American Chargé d'Affaires and Sir Philip, and now the Porte says it was all a mistake, and they may remain.

Our passports to the interior have been issued by the English Consulate and are now waiting to be signed by the Turkish authority—we, and every one here, quite hope that it will soon come all right. If any difficulty is made, Sir P. Currie told R. to let him know at once.

Last night our dear friends here invited a very interesting company to meet us. Several Armenians were of the number, one a Protestant pastor named Kapriolian— who is called here "the Armenian Spurgeon"—who told us that the troubles have drawn the Old Armenian Church and themselves into the closest sympathy, and that the Bishop of Scutari (the "Catholicos") said to him recently, "We have misunderstood you in the past, but now we are brothers and can never again be separated;" this in itself is great gain. Mr. and Mrs. Greene were here, and Mr. Cobb, the head of the British Post Office. Mr. Greene is head of all the Presbyterian Missions in Asia Minor, and father of the author of that book on Armenia which has been so much read in England; Miss Armitage of the Sailors' Rest, Mrs. White, matron of the English Hospital, and the minister of the English Church previously referred to, and many others, were present. At the close of the evening R. read the 91st Psalm, and then said that our faith in God would not fail us at this time *if* we all of us gave ourselves continually to be His instruments, or as R. put it, "lesser providences," for the help of the Armenians. Only those people who did nothing should despair. Then we had an open time of prayer, and several took part very earnestly.

I have now brought our movements up to date, and as Dr. Long of Robert College is coming here directly to take us to see the Museum I will say good-bye.—Yours affectionately,

HELEN B. H.

P.S.—The weather is cold now again and wet, and we are glad of warm clothing.

P.S.—4.30 P.M. The matter of our permit for travel has now gone up to the Grand Vizier, and they say they hope to give us not only the ordinary teskerch, but a special one which will insure us particular attention wherever we go! The special Providences which have led up to this have been most remarkable, and especially this afternoon. We shall now see about a dragoman and other things. Dr. Long went with R. to the Sublime Porte, and afterwards took us over the Museum, which is wonderful.

[As the interview with the Armenian Patriarch Izmirlian recorded in the foregoing letter was of special interest, I subjoin more extended memoranda of the conversation.—J. R. H.

The interview was a very painful one; the Patriarch showed great agony of mind for his people, and opened his heart freely to his visitors. He expressed deep gratitude for English sympathy and charitable aid sent to his starving and suffering folk, and prayed that a higher and spiritual blessing might be poured out upon the Armenian people by thus coming into contact with Christian England. Pointing to letters on his desk, he continued, "The terrible tales of torture and massacre which I receive are too heart-rending," adding, with great animation, "the whole Armenian nation is steeped in blood. It is impossible to grasp the fact that six great Christian Powers of Europe could look at these terrible massacres with folded arms. It is my firm belief that God, at any rate, will hold the stronger Christian nations responsible for the defenceless Christians butchered in cold blood." Surely England, who forty years ago could find allies to save the Turk, and who later on could tear up the San Stefano Treaty, could, if she would, intervene to rescue an ancient Christian nation, which had clung to its faith for fifteen centuries, though surrounded by foes, and for whose safety England had expressly stipulated. There was no parallel in history for such systematic and continuous persecution—by robbery, torture, imprisonment, exile, and murder—of men, women, and children, going on for years. "There have been Neros who appeared and flooded the world with blood like big waves, and then disappeared; but our suffering has no respite, no end." Asked if he approved of the idea of emigration for the Armenians, the Patriarch replied, "Yes, if it could be done nationally, not if it is to break us up. We have stood so long, and suffered so much together, that we will stand together to the end, whether that end be a free Armenia, or a common home in some other country, or extermination." After being assured of the strong feeling in England that something must be done, the Patriarch said it was his belief that God would make the nations feel their great responsibility, and that they, and England especially, would of themselves demand a final settlement. He felt comforted by so much sympathy shown and so much practical help rendered by the English, and said at parting, with solemnity, "I wish to convey my heartfelt thanks to those who have shown such deep interest and great activity in sending help to the helpless. . . . After all, we are all brothers and sisters united in Christ Jesus, and it has seemed good in God's sight that while the Armenians are passing through such terrible sufferings, I should be in the position of a shepherd of this branch of the Christian Church."]

LETTER No. III.

ARRIVAL OF THE "TESKEREH"—THE NEWLY DISCOVERED
SIXTH-CENTURY GOSPELS.

CONSTANTINOPLE, *April* 6, 1896.

DEAR FRIENDS, — The *teskereh*, or passport, arrived yesterday afternoon, too late for us to catch the steamer, but we were so thankful to have it, there was no room in our hearts for disappointment. It is worded very nicely, giving command that we shall have every assistance in travelling, even to food. How this will work out practically remains to be seen, meanwhile we are much encouraged.

Nothing else of moment has happened since I last wrote. The apprehension of the Sultan's order for all American missionaries to withdraw from Asia Minor hangs like Damocles' sword over the heads of all English and Americans here. It is now *known* to be his design, and it is said also to be the wish of the Russian Government, but perhaps this is not true.

The Russian Ambassador sent a message to R. on Friday last by Mr. Lister,[1] that he would be glad to show him the newly acquired Greek New Testament

[1] Mr. Lister is an attaché of our Embassy, and a brother of Lord Ribblesdale.

MS., for which £1000 has been given, and a Church is to be built. As this is the same one R. nearly purchased himself four years ago, and has mourned for ever since, he was of course delighted at the invitation.[1] Mr. Lister also told R. that the Ambassador had said to him, that he had had a letter from Prince Lobanoff with reference to our journey, asking him to help in any way he could. When R. went to the Russian Embassy several Russian Professors were examining the book, but it was at once put into his hands. The critical results of this examination will of course be tabulated elsewhere. When R. left, the Ambassador took him aside and privately expressed his sympathies. This kindness is of course the result of our friend Edmund Brooks' interest at St. Petersburg.

We are not sure what day we shall get off. We have to lay in supplies for the journey, as it seems a great risk as well as expense to take a proper dragoman, at least from here, but we shall leave by the first steamer of any sort.—Affectionately your friend,

HELEN B. H.

[1] A purple vellum MS. of the Gospels written in gold and silver letters. Stray leaves of it were already in the great European libraries (Rome, Vienna, London, and in the island of Patmos). The book has for a long time been in process of diminution, from various causes. The people of the village confided to me that when their bishop came amongst them he always had this book to pray with, and they implied that the leaves grew fewer as the prayers grew more numerous. Its curative value was also great. You soak a leaf in water, and give the liquid to the patient to drink !—J. R. H.

LETTER No. IV.

PROJECTED DEPARTURE FROM SMYRNA TO ALEXANDRETTA — AN AMERICAN LADY MISSIONARY FROM THE INTERIOR — POSSIBILITY OF ARMENIAN EMIGRATION.

SMYRNA, *April* 12, 1896.

MY DEAR FRIENDS,—I have nothing much to add to the news which Helen has already communicated, but as we expect to leave to-morrow in a little Greek steamer for Alexandretta, and this is the last place where our letters will have the protection of a British post-office, I think I had better take the opportunity and report what we are doing.

As we draw nearer and nearer to the places where our call takes us, the accounts become more distressing. We have met here a young lady missionary from Ourfa, who was the companion and helper of Miss Shattuck, the heroine of that place, who has borne all the burden and heat of the day. Miss M. is from Iowa, and an American in every respect; keen and active, as rapid as a rotifer, or whatever those little creatures are that dart about under the microscope; she is a very interesting Christian, and is only waiting for permission to return to the place where she has been labouring for the last five years.

She was in Ourfa until before the great massacres; at that time they were caring for some thousands of refugees who had made their way on foot from Moush (nearly fifteen days' journey), and had arrived in extreme destitution, with their bodies, as she says, a mass of corruption. From these people Miss M. took the fever, and after some weeks, during which she was unconscious, and was nursed by Miss S., who never left her for more than two hours at a time, she recovered, and eventually was able to come to Smyrna. She says she is all the better for having had this dispensation, and would come on with us at once if the American Board would let her, and the Turks give her the necessary pass. But both of these are withheld at present, and perhaps it is all right, for she is doing good service here in digesting written communications which come from the interior, and sending her copies and translations westward. We have arranged for her to send some of her letters to our friends in England. So you must imagine a bright American Western girl, with her hair just growing afresh on her head after the fever, and as full of enthusiasm for Christ and the people of Christ as a whole platform of Exeter Hall people.

I begin to see that the deeds of Christian heroism which have gone on here, and are still going on, equal anything in the pages of Eusebius (indeed much of it is very like his account of the Martyrs of Palestine in the ninth book of the Ecclesiastical History). Also it is clear that things are far worse than we thought; perhaps the destitution has reached the point where it is hopeless to help except by emigration. We hear that from several provinces the Armenians have petitioned the Sultan either to give them the means of re-tilling their fields, or to let them leave the country, or to send his soldiers back again to put them out of their misery.

We are thinking much on the second head. It looks as absurd as if one proposed to dig up Armenia and carry it away. I had a long talk yesterday with a rich American railroad king, who was passing through Smyrna, on one of the French steamers. He almost promised to take some thousands of Armenians, if I could get them to New York, and locate them in the Western States. Whether anything will come of it, it is hard to predict. But perhaps something like this would have to be done, and we might have to go to the Government about it. It would not cost more than an ironclad, perhaps.[1] However, on these things we must not say more at present; only we must be on our guard against acquiescing in hopeless misery, or giving help where it does not really dispel the distress. We shall know more about this when we get a little nearer to the scene of action.

You will probably have seen by the papers that the Turks have stopped the relief in Harpoot, and proposed to take over the relief funds and distribute them by a local committee of their own. I saw the telegrams, which arrived in Constantinople just before we left. They came from Mr. Gates, who is one of the American missionaries, if I remember rightly.[2] Mr. Whittall, the chairman of the Constantinople Committee, was sending them on to the ambassador, and I have no doubt that

---

[1] Unfortunately a Government that operates, not to destroy men's lives but to save them, has not yet appeared.

[2] This interference with the relief work was afterwards abandoned.—J. R. H.

immediate pressure will be put on the officials who are so zealously disposed towards the new virtue of charity (but to whom?). Sir Philip Currie has done a great deal of noble work in this crisis, and must not be condemned for the sins of Lord Beaconsfield, whose policy he has to follow. He is almost the only person in Constantinople who has stood for justice, and has often made himself heard and obeyed.

We have met with astonishing kindness from people of all nationalities and all classes in society. The poorer Armenians in Constantinople seem to have had an inkling of our business, and they have been helpful to us in many little ways. One young man who came to help me bargain for a quilt from a Turkish shop, replied to my thanks for a successful encounter between the buyer and seller, by saying, not "backsheesh," but "it is nothing, it is for our people." And this is only a little specimen of a great deal of kindness that has been showered upon us. The wonder is that the Turkish spies, who are everywhere, have not laid their hands upon us. But, so far, we seem to have escaped.

This evening Helen is going to address a meeting at the Sailors' Rest. We found a friend of ours in charge of this work, a Miss Turnely from Ireland; her brother is also here, engaged in educational mission work. It is very pleasant to find so many of our people everywhere; it makes home nearer, travelling easier, and the world of a smaller radius; and all these advantages are prized by us. The last of them is not the least: it is easier to believe in the unity of humanity in a moderate-sized world than in a very large one; and I have had lately a keen feeling of the strong natural ties which defy the severing influences of races and of religions.

Our love with this to all our friends in England. Letters will come now more slowly. God bless you all.

J. R. H.

LETTER No. V.

ARRIVAL AT ALEXANDRETTA—START FOR THE INTERIOR.

KHAN, ALEXANDRETTA, *April* 18, 1896.

DEAR FRIENDS,—The second stage of our journey from Constantinople here has now been safely accomplished, and we are landed here with the Custom House behind our backs. We had a rather trying voyage from Smyrna, as we were obliged to take a little Greek coasting steamer, the alternative being a ten days' wait. We had every attention from captain and steward, but the little vessel rolled and pitched, and loitered in several little harbours, and we neither of us proved as impervious to these circumstances as might have been wished. Nevertheless we were glad to be on board, and now we are *very glad* to be on land again.

We hear from the American Consul here (the British Consul being at Aleppo, we are thrown on the help of the former) that the country is very disturbed, and he considers our journey a very risky one; but as we knew this before, of course it makes no difference.

We are now negotiating for a servant as far as Aintab, and may start this afternoon. The man under special consideration is a Greek. We hear that two of the Red Cross workers have gone to Marash, where the need is so great; two others are at Ourfa, and we may meet them there: I hope we shall.

The big turret-warships in the beautiful little harbour here look very out of keeping with the lovely scenery—grand snow-capped mountains all around, and such a blue calm sea!

Near our little khan the hubbub is indescribable. The usual Moslem crowd of every hue and dress, and I have just had to close the shutter in front of this table where I am writing, because two Turkish women were flattening their faces against the window to get a good look in.

Our *teskereh* (Turkish passport) does not appear to be an unusual one after all—so Dr. D——'s servant, who first interpreted it for us, must have romanced a little—it does, however, recommend us to ordinary attention.

We feel much peace in being here, and believe we are not alone. Please continue to pray for us, for we need help in this way very much, and shall do.

Mr. Knapp, the American missionary from the interior, who is charged with inciting to rebellion (no doubt because he showed active sympathy with the poor Armenians), and who is to be tried at Constantinople, is expected here to-day *en route,* so we may see him. I honour him very much.

R. joins with me in love to all our dear friends, and I remain, ever yours affectionately,

HELEN B. H.

Postscript.

KILLIS, *April* 22.

We left Alexandretta yesterday punctually at 6 A.M., and with a carriage for ourselves, a waggon for our luggage and the servant, and two *zaptichs* to guard us, we set out. The drive was first over the dangerous malarial plain, then up beautiful mountain steeps and passes, with constant glorious views, and the purest air, and as the day was showery in its first hours, a lovely rainbow seemed to travel with us, which we took as an omen of promise for our journey. After a while we descended again by a long and beautiful zig-zag, with a capital road and most lovely flowers skirting the way, anemones in profusion, &c. Below us was an outstretched lake with marshy land, but when we reached the shore we found a very different climate, &c., from A.—the most luxuriant country, the richest pasturage, delicious streams, half covered with a lovely white water-flower, immense herds of sheep, camels, buffalo, and also horses, and the road one constant stream of caravans; hundreds and hundreds of camels, crowds of donkeys, and multitudes of pack-horses. The traffic between Alexandretta and Aleppo must be something enormous to sustain such a stream of trade.

All along the plain the agriculture seemed far more prosperous than we had expected; magnificent sweeps of growing corn and grazing land, and later, fig and olive orchards and some vines, but a far richer country than Palestine—the soil seemed extremely rich, and as if it could never be exhausted.

From time to time, we saw very curious looking mounds

rising from the plain; R. says that they probably cover

ruined cities, and that there was once a very fine civilisation here.

We had four relays of soldiers each day, and it was very amusing to notice their different characters. Seven out of the eight of yesterday had good horses, and all were gaily dressed and carried a gun over their shoulders. They salaamed when they first came, and came for backsheesh before leaving, between which processes, they carried out their ideas of guardianship differently. Several rode close by our carriage window all the time, frequently looking in, I suppose to see that we had not fallen out by the way. Some caracolled off, and kept quite at a distance in front or behind, and one actually threw a rose in at the window. Our journey yesterday was about forty odd miles, and at its close we stayed at a khan—such a place as I never was in before—absolutely nothing but four bare walls,—fancy, after such a journey! Our servant, whose name is Griva, and a young Armenian who had attached himself to our party, did what they could, but altogether one realised as never before, I think, some of the conditions of primitive existence.

We passed immense beds of asphodel in the plains, and also the liquorice plant. At Hammam, Rendel had a bath in a hot sulphur stream, and felt much the better for it.

To-day we journeyed about thirty miles, and reached this most Oriental city. We were first taken to the great khan, where our coming caused tremendous excitement; afterwards, we came to a quiet Greek home, and were thankful for Mr. Aristides' kind hospitality. He is factor to Mr. Walker at A., and we carried a letter to him which insured a welcome. We found on coming here that there were a hundred men killed on the 20th March, and that about fifty are still suffering from wounds then received. There seem to be several influential Turkish families here, who did what they could to prevent bloodshed. We saw a young doctor from Beyrout, who is doing what he can, but he told us of many horrors, especially of hands cut off, which seems a common form of brutality in these outbreaks.

LETTER No. VI.

JOURNEY TO AINTAB—TROUBLES AT KILLIS—AN EARLY START BAULKED—A HARD NIGHT—ARRIVAL AT AINTAB.

AINTAB, *April* 23, 1896.

WE have just arrived here, and find that there is a post going seaward to-day, so I catch the opportunity to send word where we are. The last four days have been occupied in continuous travel, and we are somewhat the worse for wear.

We rode two days in a carriage, engaging a waggon or *araba* for our servants and bags of needment. By this means, as the roads were at their best, we made forty miles odd on Monday and nearly as many on Tuesday, and finished the two days' journey at Killis, which you will remember as the scene of the latest massacre some three weeks or so ago; we thus found ourselves in the wake of the storm, and were able to form some idea of what it must have been like. The Armenian church was turned into a hospital, and I was told that there were seven men still lying there, several of whom cannot survive. As it is no part of my business to officiously thrust myself into the political life of the country, I did not indulge the sightseer's natural instinct to look at anything that has the flavour of death or dying, and no doubt my conduct would in this way be more acceptable to the authorities; for I gathered that the *kaimakam* or mayor does not approve of such visits being made, and I do not think he would wish an interior view of the church to be taken, nor that an "interview" (in the modern sense) should be sought with sufferers and doctors.

We had great trouble in getting away from Killis. I ordered our horses to start at six, and was up at five myself to superintend operations, but no horses appeared, and only after a long while two or three sorry mules. We had a solid fight with the Killisians for two hours and a half, and succeeded in getting the anchor up (please notice my Greek love of the sea, and how it deranges my metaphors) by 8.30 of the clock.

The consequences of all this delay were apparent in the afternoon, when we were informed by the policeman or *zaptieh* who had us in charge, that it was unsafe to push through to Aintab, as the road was infested with Circassians and robbers, and that we must put up for the night at a village khan. My dear friends will regard it as a historical benediction on their lives that they have never had to sleep in such quarters; it was an alternation of conflicts with savage men and brute beasts of minute dimension; but I think I had better leave Helen to describe our horrible night, the attempt that was made to break in upon us, and the general sense of savagery around.[1] I don't think we ever slept less or found a night longer, or were more glad of daylight and ready to jump up from the floor where we

[1] This letter has apparently been lost.—J. R. H.

were lying and thank God that it was five o'clock and time to be off.

And now to-day we have crept on somewhat wearily and painfully to the great American college at Aintab, and are enjoying the luxury of the bath and the hospitality of the kindest of hosts, Dr. and Mrs. Fuller.

So now you have us placed on the map: in your prayers also we are sensibly well-placed, even though perhaps on your side it may sometimes seem as difficult to pray intelligently as if we were Robinson Crusoe, and cast on a lonely island. To such places love understands the navigation.

J. R. H.

LETTER No. VII.

AMERICAN BRAVERY—OFFICIAL HYPOCRISY AND FATALISM—DETAILS OF THE GREAT MASSACRE—INSULTS TO ENGLAND—OCCUPATIONS OF ARMENIAN WOMEN—SOME COMPASSIONATE TURKS, ETC.

DR. FULLER'S HOUSE, AMERICAN COLLEGE,
AINTAB, *April* 24, 1896.

DEAR FRIENDS,—The interest here is so deep, and the things we are hearing and seeing every hour so remarkable, that if I can only convey a *hundredth* part to you of what we have been made to feel and think, I shall be glad.

And first let me say that words can never express the welcome and kindness we have received here, nor our wonder at the possibility of such an establishment and work existing amidst such absolutely antagonistic surroundings. Here is a noble building with extensive grounds, tennis-court, president's and professors' houses, and in a word peace, culture, Christianity, courtesy, education, surrounded by four strong walls, with a porter's lodge, and outside anarchy, fanaticism, and confusion reign. Dr. and Mrs. F., the joint directors of this grand work, each in their own sphere are worthy of their position, and nothing dismayed or daunted because the Turkish Government has demanded their dismissal as seditious persons. (The request, I need hardly say, was not favourably received by the United States Embassy, and so they are here still.)

To show how bravely they face their position, I must mention one incident which specially shows Mrs. F.'s character. Lately her husband had escorted some lady missionaries to Alexandretta, and the Governor of Aintab took the opportunity to demand the surrender of the senior professor here, a noble, elderly Armenian gentleman (who spent an hour with us yesterday evening). The Turks had tried to get him before and had been refused, and now they thought, the Dr. being absent, was their time! So an official arrived one morning with a document from the Governor and politely asked Mrs. F. who was her husband's deputy? She replied that *she was*, when with many regrets he presented his paper. She looked at it, and said such a request was impossible to comply with. He demanded and urged his authority, but she simply said "No,"—she would go herself if need be, but give up the Professor—never! So the official returned the way he came, and they have heard no more of the matter. This Professor has his home within fifteen minutes' walk of the college, but he has not ventured outside the walls for six months. Nor indeed do any of the Armenian collegians venture out, nor for three months did any one.

There are a number of interesting looking people on the grounds here, who have lost their own homes. They all seem patient and doing their best to be trustful and hopeful.

One lady had her harmonium and sewing-machine

smashed up before her eyes, but the loss of such things is trifling compared to their other losses, and her husband is in prison at Aleppo. Some of the marauders, when they find they cannot use the things they stole at the time of the massacre here, are bringing them back and selling them boldly to their former owners! There were about 300 killed here, November 16, 1895, and numbers mutilated, hands and right arms cut off, and eyes gouged out, to render the poor people helpless. Dr. F. says when they first got among these, the day after the massacre, it was awful hearing them crying for death to end their sufferings.

The same day he went to the Governor's house, where he sat surrounded by his satellites, and when Dr. F. came in they were very polite and said, "Ah! How terrible this is! Our town is all broken to pieces, but what can we do? God wills it."[1] At the very same moment of these lamentations, the best rugs and other furniture of the looted houses were being safely conveyed to their own homes, where they were afterwards seen and recognised.

One of the cruel ways of outraging Christian feeling, as well as of maltreating the bodies of the sufferers here and

[1] Any attempt to dispute this fatalistic statement is met by the inquiry, "Does anything happen without God?" If we cannot directly meet the question (and indeed the only way to meet it is to suggest that some other things will happen presently "with God"), we can at least detect in the form of this question a survival from an earlier theology than the Turkish. For in the Teaching of the Twelve Apostles we are told to receive the things that come upon us as good — *knowing that without God nothing happens!* There must have been a streak of fatalism in the Early Church. All Eastern Churches preserve traces of it.—J. R. H.

elsewhere, was to slash them twice across the breast in the form of the cross, and say, "Where is your Christ now? Where is your Jesus? Why does He not save you." After the massacre the Turks got a panic that the English were going to come and punish them, and many went to the Armenians they knew, and said, "You know we did not let you be killed, (?) now you must shelter us."

This change of feeling passed again, when it was found that no English came, and then, *several times* they led a donkey with a mangy dog tied on its back around the town, amid great uproar and scorn, and cries of "Make way for Queen Victoria!" They also had a somewhat similar demonstration in derision of the Christ, who they said could not save the Armenians any better than Queen Victoria. Apropos of the scare of the English coming to punish them, some of these Turks got up a report that an artesian well, which was being dug at the time on the College grounds, was *an underground way to England*, and that soon English soldiers would come up from its depths and destroy the town! Others said it was not an underground way to *England*, but to *America itself*.

We have now had some opportunity of seeing the Armenians themselves, both of the higher and lower classes. The Professors here and their wives and families are the top of the tree, and probably of the finest type and education to be found in the country, and as they have spent a good part of two evenings here in Mrs. F.'s drawing-room with us, and there has been no lack of conversation, we have become pretty well acquainted. They all speak English excellently and talk with great interest and intelligence of the situation: indeed I see no inferiority on their part to Europeans, and they are a fine set of men physically as well as intellectually.

'Yesterday Mrs. S., the wife of Dr. Shephard (just returned from Zeitun and Marash with the English Consul, Mr. Barnham), took me to a number of poor homes in the town, from which husbands, sons, &c., have been taken by the recent trouble, either by death or to be put in prison. Mrs. S. is employing a number, about two hundred, of these men and women in embroidery, a most exquisite industry to which they seem born, and the results of which she is sending to "Liberty's," London. I want very much that some English friends of the Armenians should open a depôt for its sale, so that a mere business-firm should not absorb all the profits from this fruit of industry, every penny of which one could wish the poor women to have. From house to house we went (five or six), and in each one was the same exquisite cleanliness, great delicacy of personal neatness—their hands so fine and clean for their beautiful work—and in every home, in spite of bare walls, a plant or two, scented geranium mostly, and in every case a leaf or two was picked and presented to us both on leaving. In better homes they give a little button-hole bouquet, but you cannot call anywhere and come away flowerless! The girls here are strikingly pretty; bright brown eyes, delicately marked eyebrows, white regular teeth, and gentle manners, and their black glossy hair they wear in long braids; and these are the women the Turks are taking and treating as we know. Delicate, modest, gentle girls! Several cases we have heard of here were sad enough.

I took my "Frena" camera with me and photographed some ruined and burnt houses, but I wish I could have photographed a regular catacomb I went down into, under one house. It is being dug now by one family, in the courtyard of their house. You see the better houses are protected by high walls with iron doors outside, and a court within, and *inside the court they cannot be seen*, so they are preparing a place of refuge for any future calamity. It was a scramble getting down, some ten feet underground; but once there they had already made a good cave, very much indeed like some of the chambers in the Catacombs at Rome. This catacomb is connected with the well, so that in case of detention they would have water. I took the opportunity of telling them of the early Christians who had suffered at Rome and acted much as they were doing now, at the same time expressing my earnest hope that their catacomb might never be used.

When one of the large Christian houses was attacked and fired, some one called out for the water-hose to put out the fire, and a man ran to seek it. It was sent attached, *not to water*—but a *petroleum* barrel, and so the fire was helped instead of hindered. The lady of this house and her son were both shot as they came out—offering to give the mob anything they wanted—and their bodies burned.

I do not mean to put many tales of horror into my letters, but one more I must add just now, as it was told on the lawn-tennis ground yesterday, by one of the students to a horrified group of his companions, and then interpreted to me. One of their own number, a hot-headed young fellow, had left the college at the time of the Zeitun excitement, with the idea of helping his fellow-countrymen there. News had just come in that he had died in prison, and on his dead foot the marks were found where a red-hot horse-shoe had been fastened.

Now for a change. It will do your hearts good to know that all the Turks are not cruel. The American hospital here would undoubtedly have been wrecked but for the determined efforts of a Turk, whose brother's life Dr. S. had saved. Other Turks also secreted Christian friends and neighbours in their houses. The Armenians themselves are helping one another splendidly.[1] Everywhere this is the case. It is not only England and America that have given money. Many rich Armenians have quite impoverished themselves, and they are waiting on the sick and caring for the homeless in the church and school-houses here most lovingly.

This letter is so long I must now draw to a close, though

---

[1] In verification of this statement, here is a little table of contributions in money and goods made at Aintab between November 16, 1895, and March 8, 1896, the values being given in piastres :—

Cereals	13,000	Bread, &c.	350
Wheat	12,100	Shoes, &c.	250
Lentils	2,050	Soap	120
Molasses	1,025	Clothes and unmade material	30,220
Raisins	2,250		
Salt	125	Bedding	1,560
Charcoal	1,120	Alaja	2,152
Wood, &c.	515	Ornaments (gold and silver)	3,145
Butter	513	Cash	31,123
Olive oil	100		
Meat	2,560	Total	104,548
Vegetables	270		= £T. 829

from which it appears that the conjunction of "deep poverty" and "riches of liberality" still exists.—J. R. H.

I have already enough more facts to tell to fill several letters. Yesterday the English Consul, who has been at Zeitun for months, and Dr. S., who went over when the fever broke out there, returned together; the Consul weak from recovery from typhus just gone through. All this morning he was in the drawing-room receiving visitors. The Turkish Governor of Aintab came to see him; then came the General of the Turkish army in Asia Minor and his aide-de-camp, now staying here; and after they left an archbishop, and the Protestant head of the Y.M.C.A. here, an Armenian gentleman educated in America and England. What contrasts, and what phases of life all these men represented you can imagine as well as I—but R. and I sat through all the visits and shook hands with all the men, though I did not enjoy the operation with the Turks. Still these are only the tools used—not the responsible arch-schemer and commander of the tragedy—and one pitied more than anything else, while looking and listening, and watching them smoking, drinking coffee, eating sweetmeats, and laughing.

Since then I have gone over the hospital, have seen the tears running down the cheeks of a strong man paralysed for life by cruelty, as he told of all his family and friends being killed but himself; there was also a poor woman from Ourfa whose hand was nearly cut off. She brightened up a little when I said I was going to her city, and sent her "salaams" to her son of fourteen, and to Miss Shattuck.

To-morrow we shall have a wonderful day. It is the day of prayer for Armenia in England, and the commencement here of a week of services. The great Gregorian Church, which holds when full over three thousand people, will be packed twice, once at daybreak for men, when a special service of ritualistic prayer will be held, and then Dr. Fuller and R. are to speak; and at noon it is to be filled again with the women (such a thing as never happened before), for me to read the letter I have from the Women's Armenian Relief Committee and speak, and also a letter of sympathy from America is to be read to them. The Gregorian priests belonging to the Church are to be present, and the Protestant minister, a professor of the college, will conduct the meeting and interpret, but no other men. At the same time a children's meeting will be held in another church.

In the afternoon R. is to speak at the Protestant Church, and in the evening both of us at the College Service. Three weeks ago these meetings and services would have been utterly impossible, so you see how wonderful has been the *leading* that has brought us here for the opening of this week of services and prayer, and of which we knew nothing.—Yours affectionately,

HELEN B. H.

[As it is interesting to know the grounds upon which the attempt (alluded to in the foregoing letter) was made to expel Dr. Fuller from the country, I subjoin a part of a communication from him, dated August 19, 1896, which will show how causeless and unjust was the agitation against the Americans.—J. R. H.

The week in Aintab has been very quiet, but it has brought to a culmination a characteristic incident which will be of interest to all who are watching the progress of affairs in this country, viz.: The first massacre and plundering at Ourfa occurred October 25–27; Miss Shattuck was at that time the only member of our Mission in Ourfa. While the mob were yet murdering and plundering her neighbours, she sent a letter to us at Aintab by special messenger, who delivered the message October 26; on November 1, as he was returning, I gave him a note to Miss S. in reply. This man was arrested at Biredjik, his papers taken from him, and himself tried and condemned as a spy. It was immediately and loudly heralded that a letter written by the president of the college had fallen into the hands of the police, and that it contained undeniable and damning proof of the complicity of the missionaries with political agitators. This report was industriously circulated at Aintab and Ourfa, and was made a matter of repeated and formal complaint to our Consul at Aleppo by the Vali. As I was wholly ignorant of what particular letter might be referred to, I could only give and authorise a general protestation of innocence, with a challenge to produce any letter bearing my signature to which the Government could rightfully object; I especially wrote our Consul, Mr. Poche, authorising him to make the most explicit and positive denial of any and all political interference or intrigue on my part, and requesting him to demand from the Vali copies of any objectionable documents bearing my signature which might be in his possession, and offering to come personally to Aleppo to explain or to answer for anything which might cause anxiety to the Government in any word or act of mine. This method of adjusting affairs did not, however, meet the approval of his Excellency; the charges against us as a mission were persistently kept alive, and chiefly on the strength of the feeling aroused by this mysterious letter, two petitions, one signed by the present Governor and some of the principal officials of Aintab, and another quite widely signed by citizens, and representing the college as a pestilent centre of political intrigue, and the missionaries generally as highly objectionable persons, and requesting their immediate expulsion from the country, were sent to Aleppo and Constantinople. On the return of our Ambassador from America the matter was taken in hand, and a copy of the famous letter was demanded and finally furnished. I take pleasure in adding a copy, and commend it to all who have occasion to send messages in Turkey, as a specimen of what is here regarded as "seditious."

AINTAB, *Nov.* 1, 1895.

DEAR MISS SHATTUCK,—Your letter received. We are in the deepest anxiety about you, especially as we get no further news; we are doing all in our power to secure influences for your protection.

When your letter came Dr. S. and Mr. S. were both away. Dr. S. came last night, but it does not seem possible for any one to get through to Ourfa in the present state of things. Brother S. will be here Saturday or Monday, and we will do all in our power to reach you. Be sure we think of you, and pray for you every moment. The situation here is very critical, but so far there has been no outbreak. Dr. S. and Mrs. Fuller send much love, as would all in our circle if they knew of this letter going.—Very sincerely yours,

       (Signed) A. FULLER.]

LETTER No. VIII.

AMERICAN CIVILISATION IN THE MIDST OF TURKISH DESOLATION—
REVIVAL OF RELIGION IN AINTAB—REMARKABLE SERVICES IN
THE OLD GREGORIAN AND PROTESTANT CHURCHES.

AINTAB, *April* 27, 1896.

I MUST not delay to write and tell you how increasingly interesting our work here is becoming, and how wonderfully the way is being made before us. We are much impressed by what we see here, both as regards the conflict between civilisation and barbarism, and as regards the religious emancipation of the people from their ancient superstitions. We are staying here at the American College, which has been doing a great work in this part of Turkey, and is naturally much hated by those who are fanatically inclined amongst the Moslems. It is an unspeakable comfort to be landed in this oasis, where one can enjoy for a little while the comforts and conveniences of Western life. Will it sound strange to hear that in Aintab I play tennis with the professors and students of the college, and that last night we had some passages from the *Messiah* sung for us? If it surprises you, it is equally strange to us, who were quite unprepared to find how fast things have been moving here in the last few years. No wonder the authorities are alarmed, as they see the old order passing away, and feel their supremacy disintegrating from day to day. But enough of this; I only want to impress upon you the fact that Armenia is very little understood as far as relates to its place in civilisation, for the simple reason that its place is changing so rapidly.

You must imagine us then as living in a beautiful American house in the midst of the college grounds. We look across the valley to the American Hospital and the Girls' Seminary, behind which is the city with its minarets. On the left the old Arab castle, which appears to be rebuilt from an earlier structure of the Crusaders. If that is right, as I think it is, the view comprises the obsolete chivalry of Western Christendom, the decaying barbarism of Islam, and the rush of advancing progress from beyond the sea. A singular combination! One moment the eye rests upon the burnt ruins of the massacre of last November, the next upon the towers and parapets which tell of the battles of the mediæval world, and side by side the splendid buildings which represent the missionary impulse and the philanthropy of the nineteenth century.

But what I want to tell you most of is the remarkable religious phenomena that are before us here. The first result of all these horrible massacres has been to draw together the various bodies of Christians, and to accomplish a religious unity such as no councils could ever have found a basis for. I think I mentioned in one of my previous letters that an Armenian Protestant pastor in Constantinople had said to me, in view of the reconciliation that was going on between the Protestants and the old Armenian Church, that it would not be long before the evangelical preachers would be occupying the old churches. But I certainly hardly expected to see this so soon fulfilled, still less to be myself a small factor of the fulfilment. But here in Aintab the thing is an accomplished fact; and when I tell you of it you will, I am sure, be astonished, and praise God. Yesterday my wife and myself preached to audiences of about 11,000 people, and this alone is sufficient to make the day one of the most memorable in our lives.

The way it comes about is something like this: it is the result of three operating factors. First, the solidifying influence of an awful persecution; the same cause which brought in the early Christian Church the orthodox and the so-called heretic before the same tribunal, and often resulted in the canonisation of the heretic along with the orthodox (as in the case of Perpetua and Felicitas, and other well-known martyrs), has been at work here; and the Christians here have been wonderfully drawn together by the trials through which they have had to pass. As one of the pastors said to me to-day, "We were like pieces of cold iron, but this persecution has welded us together." The second cause which has been at work is the sympathy of Western Protestant Nonconformity. The Armenians know very well how much of sympathy has come to them from the old English and American Evangelicals, and they have drawn their own conclusions. They say: "We understand the Protestants now, and know that they are not heretics." And thirdly, since the alleviation of the sufferings of the people has largely flowed through the hands of the native Armenian pastors, working with the old Gregorian Armenians, the two poles of religious thought and life have been brought into such contiguity that sparks of material love have been passing all the time. No doubt other and higher influences have also been at work which do not admit of classification under firstly, secondly, and thirdly, because they are above all, and through all, and in all. Well, one result of this upheaval in Aintab has been that the Protestants (including the college professors and native preachers) have been preaching the Gospel in the old Gregorian Church, and in the very midst of the old Gregorian ritual.

The people, too, in the midst of their sorrows, have turned their attention to religion in a way that has probably never been known before. All the churches are crowded, generally twice a day, and the people will sit for hours listening to the consolations of the kingdom of God. Yesterday, as I said, was our great day. Dr. Fuller, president of the American College, had been invited to preach at the Gregorian High Mass, and he obtained permission for me to come and share the privilege with him. It was the first time he had ever had the opportunity, and the first time I had been in anything of the kind. The service began before daybreak, and as the ritual is extremely long, and without any preaching occupies about two hours, you can judge what it would be like with a couple of Protestant addresses intercalated in it.

I was out of bed by ten minutes after five, and after a cup of coffee and a bit of bread we were soon on our way

to the church, where we found the service already well
advanced. But what a sight! From end to end of the
building a sea of heads; the men stood, of course, as there
are no seats, but only carpets on the floor, and I need not
say that the capacity of a building is vastly increased when
the people stand or when they sit close packed upon the
floor; away in the galleries and behind lattice-work was
a throng of women, and a glance overhead at the lantern
showed that a crowd of women were also listening on
the roof. I suppose there must have been 3000 people
present, and they say that another thousand was in the
courtyard and unable to get into the church. When the
first sunbeams fell on this crowd within the church, with
their red fezzes, blue jackets, and striped shirts, it made
a fantastic sea of colour that is not easy to describe. The
service is much more extended than most masses of which
I know anything. The main features of the eucharistic
method, however, were not difficult to recognise. The
Nicene Creed was recited by the whole congregation, and
the kiss of peace was given, usually by turning one's
cheeks to one's neighbours, first to the one side and then
to the other, but without any actual contact between the
lips and the face. The procession of the priests, as they
brought the elements from one altar to the other to place
them in the hands of the celebrant, was very interesting.
The approaching priest recites from the psalm, "Lift up
your heads," &c., and the celebrant inquires, "Who is
this King of Glory?" and so on, the elements being placed
on the altar. But I need not enlarge further on this
ancient ritual. Indeed I do not understand it as well as

I could wish (speaking as an archæologist). In the midst of the service one of the clergy read a paper of subscriptions for the poor, usually in the form of thanksgivings or requests for prayer, and it was very interesting to note that no less than four donations were made in thankfulness for the safe return of the American doctor (Dr. Shephard) from Zeitun. One person added, "and for the safe return of the English Consul," who had been prayed for by the people in the great church.

When it came to the time for the sermon, Dr. Fuller was introduced and preached to the people extempore; they listened with breathless attention, and often by a murmur of sympathy or by a responsive "Amen," expressed their approval of what was said. I was back in Antioch by this time with Chrysostom! Then came my turn to say a few words. After this the service continued; the elements were elevated, portions of blessed bread were distributed amongst the people, and finally the first chapter of the Gospel of John was read (in the Old Armenian, I think), and so the liturgy concluded. A short service was then commenced in commemoration of the dead, but by this time we were tired, it was eight o'clock, and most of the people were leaving. So we came back to the college with thankful hearts for the opportunity we had enjoyed of speaking of the Kingdom of God to a people who do not generally hear anything on that point, beyond the obscure intimations of the ritual.

At noon the great church was crowded again, but this time 3000 women had the floor, and my dear wife was the celebrant of the mysteries. I must leave her to give her own impressions of that remarkable service.

The afternoon was appointed for services in almost all the churches, and I promised to come and help them at the First and Second Protestant Churches, beginning with the latter, and then going on to the former. As there was likely to be a great crowd, a service was also arranged by the Protestant pastors in the old Armenian Church. Not to allow the brotherly kindness to be all on one side, the first hour of the service in the Second Protestant Church was given up to the Gregorians, who were allowed to bring their altar with them, and set it up, with a censer and other necessaries, in front of the Protestant pulpit. And when they had done their evening service the Protestant worship began. Here, again, it was a wonderful sight. The open galleries and a small part of the main floor were reserved for women; the rest was filled with a dense mass of worshippers, who filled the building long before the appointed hour, and would, to judge from their interest, have willingly stayed all day. Professor Papagian led the service and expounded the Scriptures; he then called upon me, for whom he interpreted most beautifully; and when I had done, we slipped off to the other church, and left him to preach to the people on his own account.

The First Church is a splendid building, with a waggon roof on wooden pillars—no galleries. This time the women sat on one side of the floor in a place reserved for them. Here there must have been again 3000 people; and how they listened! First of all their pastor (educated at Yale University in America) preached them a closely reasoned discourse on the necessity of progress in the interpretation of Christianity, and then I had my little say, and so we ended. My own mind was full of blessed astonishment at the things which I had seen and heard.

In the evening we had a meeting with the students of the college, to whom my wife and I both said a few words. But you may very well believe that by nightfall we were tired enough. But who would not be tired in such a service!

And now I must conclude this letter. The people of whom I have been speaking to you, are as good material as any similar audience you could gather in England. Alas! that they should be destroyed. The preachers with whom I have been working are earnest, educated, and devout. We are well and happy. The time of our coming is the right time. A few weeks ago the people could scarcely stir abroad; even now there is great danger and constant fear. But they are plucking up courage a little, and we are doing all we can to help them. Continue with us in your prayers to God for this unhappy land and this precious people.

RENDEL HARRIS.

LETTER No. IX.

CROSSING THE EUPHRATES — DRYING UP OF THE GREAT RIVER— DIFFUSION OF THE KURDS—MISS SHATTUCK, THE HEROINE OF OURFA, ETC.

OURFA, *May* 5, 1896.

MY DEAR FRIENDS,—You see we really are at last in a position to understand "that blessed word Mesopotamia," for we crossed the Euphrates last Thursday, arrived here on Saturday, and have had two or three days to look about us and take stock of the situation. We crossed the Euphrates at Biredjik, where there is now not a single Christian left: all have either been killed or embraced Islam.[1] We came across some of these unfortunate apostates, and indeed one or two were in our party, unless I am much mistaken. One man who came to Aintab wept much over his unfortunate position, and with others will take the opportunity of confessing his faith again when better times come. I fancy they will not find it so easy. Another man sends word that although, for the sake of his wife and children, and in view of his lonely situation in the country, he has embraced Islam, he keeps up morning and evening prayer secretly with his wife. Poor

---

[1] We understand that, through the influence of Vice-Consul Fitzmaurice, these forced converts have been permitted to return to their former profession.—J. R. H.

fellows! We can hardly appreciate the terror under which they live.

As we approached the Euphrates I asked Helen whether she expected to see the river dried up, alluding of course to the interpretation which many people put upon the passage in the Apocalypse, which speaks of the drying up of the great river Euphrates that the way of the kings of the East may be prepared; but I was hardly prepared to find that the suggested event had really taken place. The great river had evidently been in flood not long since, and had now shrunk to a fifth of its size; and it seemed to me easy to conclude that the drying up of the Euphrates is a regular spring phenomenon. Consequently the passage in the Apocalypse is a cipher method of saying, that when the spring floods subside a Parthian army is waiting to cross the Euphrates. So I read it as history, as so many other events in that book, and the only question is to determine the time when the invasion was actually threatened. The Parthians were the terror of the world—at least, of the Eastern world—in the century before and the century after Christ. They were on a large scale what the Kurds are to-day on a small scale.

Speaking of the Kurds, I was surprised to find how far westward they extended. Our ride from Biredjik to Ourfa took us for two days, partly over hilly, rolling country covered with flocks of sheep and goats, and partly through splendid plains covered with waving corn. But everywhere that I could see the Kurd was in possession; he was not only the nomad visiting the spring pastures, but he was the agriculturist. We spent the night at Serouj (the ancient Serug, a place in which I was much interested as being the home of one of the most famous fathers of the Syrian Church, Jacob of Serug); the city is now a mere collection of Kurdish huts, built of mud, and having the appearance of a group of beehives. And the whole of the plain was dotted over with similar ant-hills, which made one think of Africa rather than of Asia. Nothing remains of the old civilisation of this region except a series of hills or mounds covering the sites of ancient cities and villages, and no doubt rich in antiquities, if one could be permitted to excavate them.

As I said, it surprised me to see the way in which the Kurd was holding the country. The nomadic Kurd was encamped in tents with reed walls and canvas roofs by the side of the agriculturist, who was tilling the rich plain. I reckon him to be about as unvarnished a savage as one could wish to see. Their wild dogs flew at us, and would cheerfully have torn us to pieces, and the men are not much better. And the Armenian population in this country has this unvarnished savage for its nether millstone, and a certain other varnished savage for its upper millstone — an over-lord and an under-lord. Is it any wonder that they talk of leaving the country, and eagerly discuss any and every possible scheme of emigration?

Here in Ourfa we are in the city that was once the metropolis of Eastern Christianity (the home of Abgar, of Tatian, and of Ephrem), and now has become its charnel-house and sepulchre. We pass constantly by looted shops and battered doors; we talk with the widows and pity the orphans; we try amid these wrecks to keep our own faith alive, and to rekindle the faith of the suffering people of God. They are a precious people, their patience is boundless and unutterable, and their charity towards one another abundant. What has been done for them in the West has fractional moral value compared with their care for one another. If the problem of living here can be solved they will solve it; but for myself it seems to be the insoluble and impossible problem, the *reductio ad absurdum* of existence.

We are delighted with the way in which relief operations have been carried on here. Miss Shattuck, the heroine of the massacres, is the mainspring, but she has a capital local committee (of Armenians), who investigate all cases and classify them, and give help in the wisest way, so as not to multiply distress in relieving it. There is no one here now, as far as I can make out, that is starving; the trouble may recur next autumn, but for the present the people are preserved alive, and most of them are getting to work again. The weavers have been employed to make cloth for the naked, and the coppersmiths are now being set to work to supply the empty houses with the necessary cooking gear; and so gradually the broken fabric of social order is being pieced together, and the smashed machine made ready for some more revolutions. The greatest trouble ahead will perhaps be the orphans; but here also the people are taking hold of the matter for themselves, and it will not do to open orphanage operations until everything has been done that can be done in the way of finding homes for them. Some help will be needed in this direction very soon, but not immediately. We have some idea that the house we have taken, which we have rented for a year at the sum of £5 Turkish, may be useful as a preliminary shelter after we are gone, but of this we shall know better presently. There is small-pox in the city, and one case is under care at the Mission House. They do not seem to mind much about it, and have little or no idea of disinfection and similar modern ideas.

I find that the experience through which we are passing is helping me to a much better understanding of the conditions of primitive Christianity; the situation is sometimes quite Apocalyptic, and one readily comprehends the way in which those books were produced, which dealt with the secret hopes of the Kingdom of God, and with the judgments that follow after persecutors. I must tell you one little story from a Moslem quarter. There is a woman in Aintab—a Moslem who is held in high repute, whether for sanity or sanctity I hardly know (the two things ought to tend to synonym). She is reported to have gone to the mayor, and related a vision which she had of a tree growing in a vessel of water; gradually the vessel filled, and when it filled the tree fell over. The explanation is that the vessel contained the tears of the Christians. I leave you to interpret the rest, and to drop your quota in the flood.—With every good wish to my beloved friends,

J. R. H.

LETTER No. X.

A MORNING WITH MISS SHATTUCK AT OURFA.

May 6, 1896.

DEAR FRIEND H. S. NEWMAN,—At this time of distress and emergency in Armenia, it is wonderful what a work God is giving to American missionaries, and especially to the lady missionaries, to do. At Van all know of Dr. Grace Kimball and her noble and successful work. That of Miss Shattuck at Ourfa is perhaps less known, but not less heroic. She was the one help and hope of the Christian population during the massacres (her own life at one crisis being in great danger); and ever since, her house, with the mission premises and the adjoining large Protestant church, has been the centre of distribution of the charity which has flowed hither from America and England, as also from the Armenians themselves. The mission premises surround a large courtyard, and when I arrived there this morning on a brief errand, as I supposed, I found a busy scene. Here are a group of Armenians waiting to state their various needs. Here are two native women who are employed as Bible-readers. They also gather the donations from the poor people among whom they visit, so freely given for those poorer still. Some of these are not able to give more than the value of the well-known widow's mite, while others give good sums, and brides the gold coins from their dowry-strings, while last night a pair of chased gold earrings were brought in. These Bible-women, by-the-bye, find those they go to so hungry for Bible comfort, that instead of the twos and threes, as is usual, coming together, the women are crowding by the hundred, and yesterday one of the Bible-women told Miss Shattuck that in one house and courtyard alone there were as many as three hundred. As Miss S. is afraid of this attracting too much attention, she has told them not to allow such large gatherings. How different this thirst for the Gospel is to the state of things in many favoured English towns, and how it shows that God is even now bringing good out of evil.

Near these groups are a band of children, mostly orphan, and, standing a little aloof, two Turkish soldiers, who are the immediate guards of the establishment (there being twenty others a little further off); some of these go with us when we go out, and seem to take a real interest in what is going on.

Mounting the out-door stairs to the verandah, upon which open Miss Shattuck's private rooms, and entering, I find her seated amidst her Armenian Relief Committee, seven earnest, good, and reliable men of responsible positions in the town, and she is manifestly their leader and guide in all their work. Every day they thus sit in council, and consider every case of need separately, and then scatter to carry out the blessed work upon which they are engaged.

Just now, as I enter, they are considering how to send

some orphans to Smyrna, for whom the good German deaconesses there are ready to provide. They have also a letter from Mrs. Dobrashian of Constantinople, concerning her taking some more of these parentless little ones under her care, and the whole matter is carefully considered. Miss Shattuck and the committee receive numerous personal appeals daily, and she had a number of these translated to me this morning, from an appeal for a donkey from a pedlar now recovered from his wounds, who declares he is too weak for any other work, to a request to be made whole by a dying woman who thinks the committee have all power. Most of the cases are, however, from widows with children whose husbands were killed. This committee work takes about an hour. Then comes looking at needle-work, for in one of the mission rooms are many girls engaged embroidering felt, for mats and other purposes, in hope of an English market. In the church are great heaps of wool being prepared for making up into beds for the poor. This is of course cleared out every Sunday, when the church is crowded with worshippers, holding about 2000 people. One of the visitors to Miss Shattuck this morning was an Armenian gentleman who had supplied her with money before help could come from Europe, and she was returning what had been lent by him. His life had been saved by two Turkish neighbours, whose wives called on Miss Shattuck when I was present yesterday. It is needless to say that social intercourse with the Turks on such a basis is one of the bright spots in this dark picture, which are happily not wanting to relieve it in every place.

After these items of business Miss Shattuck and I, accompanied by our guard and some of the Relief Committee, went to inspect an Armenian house, kindly lent free of cost for two months, to receive orphans, until further arrangements can be made. It has been terribly battered about, and, indeed, we have not been in one Armenian house yet which does not show marks of violence; but, in spite of injury, it is a fine old house, evidently belonging to a family or families (since life is on the patriarchal basis here) of the better class. Carved marble pillars and beautifully carved woodwork on doors and shutters showed the refinement of its late occupants. The owner was with us, and told us that twenty-one of his kith and kin who had lived there with him had been killed in the massacre. Twenty-one! Just think of the desolation of his hearth and home! and of the nobility and charity of nature that could take joy in giving the scene of former happy family life to shelter the orphan children of his people. After Miss Shattuck and her helpers had decided what had to be done to put the house in order, we next proceeded to the little infirmary where the few wounded people who have neither recovered nor died yet remain. Here is a man with a great sword-gash across his face cutting the nose in two, another shot through the lungs, another with one hand off and the other wounded, &c. Miss Shattuck gives kind words and sympathising looks to each, and as she is so occupied it becomes known that she is here, and women crowd into the outer court, each with her own hope for a word and a promise from their one friend.

Here let me leave her surrounded by the needy people she loves—utterly self-forgetful and apparently incapable of fatigue, a woman full of the deepest sympathy and tenderness, and yet, as Mr. Fitzmaurice, the British Vice-Consul, said of her, possessing the most level head of any one far and near.—Sincerely thy friend,

HELEN B. HARRIS.

LETTER No. XI.

HOUSE HIRED IN OURFA—ANCIENT LEGENDS OF EDESSA—RELIEF
WORK IN THE CITY—AN ARCHÆOLOGICAL PUZZLE, ETC.

OURFA, *May* 9, 1896.

MY DEAR FRIENDS,—We are comfortably settled in a part of a house which we have hired for a year at a very modest sum. We expect to stay here some time, as this is one of the chief centres of misery that we are in search of, and when we leave, our thought is that our part of the house can be stocked with orphans (or as I amuse myself by calling them, Ourfans), of whom the city is full.

As you know, this is the ancient Edessa, the metropolis of Syrian Christianity, and in many ways the university of the early Church. It was to this city that King Abgar, according to the legend, invited Jesus Christ to escape, promising Him protection, and assuring Him that the city was small but beautiful, and large enough for two. The description is still accurate, except for the last words; Jesus Christ finds small scope here to-day as far as the goodwill of the government is concerned. It is fortunate that the letter of Christ to Abgar, which used to be preserved in the archives of the city, and was supposed to confer immunity upon it, is a forgery; for otherwise the irony of the present situation would be tremendous. It is bad enough that the people should have dreamed themselves secure under Divine protection, and then have been awakened from their fabricated safety by the rudeness of the rule which has culminated in the horrors of these last days.

Perhaps you will be interested to know that the protection supposed to be conferred by Christ's letter to Abgar was extended from Edessa to England; for the letter became an amulet or phylactery, was translated into Saxon, and as late as the last century was worn by poor countryfolk in England about their persons to keep off various ills. What a lot of superstition there is in our common blood; but the faith will outlive the superstition, and now is our time to quicken the faith of these people by giving them a higher order of phylactery; and if they gave us Abgar's letter, and a lot of other false literature, we can give them back some of the better hopes, to which they are very willing to listen.

I have been sitting this morning with the Relief Committee, composed of Miss Shattuck and her seven deacons (as I call them), investigating the cases of plundered men and helpless women and children. One begins to understand what went on in Jerusalem in the daily ministration, and how their needs were met in times of early persecution. To-day we were chiefly concerned in trying to get some of the empty shops re-opened. The artisans have no tools and the tradesmen no stock, but if there is any chance of a man re-opening his business we, *i.e.* they, look into the case to see where he can be helped. One man was a coppersmith, but his hand was cut off; what could he do?

Another man was weak from his wounds and quite unable to take up hard work again: he was willing to try his hand at some retail trade. They planned these two men to open a shop together, and gave a small sum (such a little!) to help them begin.

We do this especially in cases where the men are struggling to support large families of relations, who must otherwise come on our hands. Some of these people were, not long since, quite well off. One man before us to-day was a silversmith; at the first massacre his shop was plundered, and at the second his house. So here he is without stock, or tools, or capital; and he is working as an apprentice in another man's shop. The question is whether his tools could be bought for him for some thirty shillings or so, so that he could begin life again in his old shop. Then other cases come on. One woman wishes to mortgage her house to pay a debt that a Moslem is pressing for; that was promptly dismissed, with the remark from one of the committee that they had better ask us to import some bankers from Europe. And so we went on. I was astonished at the shrewdness shown by our native helpers, and do not think a better committee could be found anywhere.

You would be delighted at the way in which these poor people help one another. At the present time the difficulty of paying rents is pressing severely, and the poor people are collecting for the poorer. The women bring their few remaining ornaments; and to-day one woman sent her wedding dress, to be sold for her poorer sisters. I think "her spirit will have rest."

But it is impossible for me to tell you in detail what goes on in this relief work. I only want you to know that it is splendidly managed, and that you need not have any fear that the help given here will go into wrong or doubtful hands. It is all being used to set the people on their feet again; but this is no slight task, for the work of Armenian eradication has been anything but a random frenzy. The men have been taken, and, amongst the men, the strongest and ablest and wisest. Sometimes in one family you will find a score gone, and perhaps only the grandfather with a handful of children left; but I will not write more horrors or pitifulnesses than I can help.

And now I think I will conclude this little letter with something of quite a different character, something interesting to me, and perhaps not altogether uninteresting to you. If you will look in Helen Harris' translation of the Apology of Aristides, you will find that in the account of the superstitions of the Egyptians, amongst other things, they are charged with worshipping a sacred fish, whose name is Shebyta. This fish has been a great perplexity to the editors of Aristides. To begin with, the sacred fish in Egypt is the oxyrhynchus, or "pointed nose," and no such fish as Shebyta was known, except that the Arabic lexicons said there was a fish of that name in the Euphrates, and that it was brought for sale to Aleppo. But how could Aristides, the Athenian philosopher, have talked about such a fish, or credited the Egyptians with worshipping it?

I must tell you how I solved this riddle. First of all

when we crossed the Euphrates at Biredjik, and had taken up our quarters in a very dirty khan, a man brought us a large fish, something like a salmon. Something reminded me of Aristides, and I said, "What is its name?" He said, "*Shebyta.*" So here was the disputed fish placed on our table; and the Arabic Dictionary was right, for they assured me such fish were carried to Aleppo, and to Aintab, and to Ourfa.

Still this did not explain to me why the Syriac translator of Aristides should have made this fish sacred amongst the Egyptians. That part of the puzzle I solved yesterday, and the answer came in the following way. I was visiting, under guard of a Turkish soldier, the most beautiful part of Edessa, the fish-pond on the borders of which stand the Mosque of Abraham the friend of God, and a Moslem college. This college is the successor of the famous Christian school of Edessa, and the mosque, no doubt, marks the site of an ancient Christian church. The pool is full of fish, which it is prohibited under severe penalty to kill, and which every one feeds with bread and pennyworths of parched corn. Such a rush when you throw it in! They tumble over one another, and jump half out of the water. Obviously the protection and support which the fish enjoy comes from a time when they were considered sacred. So I asked my soldier what was the name of the fish, and his answer was, "In Arabic they are called *shabut.*" So here was my fish again, and the explanation of the whole riddle. The translation of Aristides *was made in Edessa,* on the borders of the sacred pool; and when the translator came to the passage dealing with Egyptian fish-worship, he substituted the Syrian sacred fish for what he found in his Greek text.

Now I hope you do not mind a taste of archæological research in place of the burdens of the people. I harden my heart this way, and it is necessary.

The people constantly ask us what is coming next. Will there be another massacre? Are we to be allowed to live? And I can only tell them that the Ethiopian has not changed his skin, nor the leopard his spots, but neither has God forgotten to be gracious. And with this I will conclude my little letter. J. R. H.

[I add a few particulars of the troubles in Edessa, for the sake of those who may not be quite familiar with the story. The best complete account is Mr. Fitzmaurice's Report to the British Government (Blue Book, Turkey, No. 5, price 2½d.).—J. R. H.

Extracts from Recent Letters (chiefly from American Missionaries).

FROM OURFA.

January 3, 1896.

I know you will be anxious for further report of the massacre. By actual count 1500 of those killed in the streets were dragged by the feet to a long trench outside of the city and there thrown in, one on top of another. Many of those you and I knew intimately, our Boys' High School teacher, nine of the priests, and our pupils' parents took refuge in the big Armenian church. There were in the church between 1500 and 2000 people. The soldiers came and entered it and were followed by other butchers, some were first killed, but most were burned. The church itself is of most solid stone and did not burn. They have been longer in cleaning up the church than in the streets. For several days I have seen men lugging in sacks the ashes, bones, &c., along the brow of the hill just by our house, and dumping the contents over the wall. The air in the city is *very bad*. I have with me in the house, church, and school-rooms 250 people, many of them seriously wounded. It takes me, with the help of the others, from five to six hours daily to dress the wounds. One woman will probably lose her arm. Each person has more than one wound. I sent to the Government and demanded 300 loaves of bread and 500 beds and clothing. Hundreds of people have come to me for shelter, but I had to turn them away, as there is no room. They come with pale, drawn faces, having lived in wells, coal-heaps, manure-heaps, and similar places, and have not tasted food for several days. The massacre was carried on systematically. One set of soldiers went ahead and killed the men, and were followed by another set who drove the women and children in crowds, and with much rough treatment, to the khans and mosques. Still another set followed, who then stripped the houses of everything.

Our pastor had a most peaceful end ; was shot and no blood ran. The six orphaned children were sent to me and are with me still.

Some of the most wealthy of our people have now nothing left in this world ; they are with me, and so humble and patient and untiring in helping me and others. Is this the answer to our hours of prayer that the Church might be purified? They have indeed passed through the fire. I am so grateful that the people here with me are so calm. We have had some very precious services among them.

March 1.

We have cut, tied up, and marked 555 garments within three or four days, and also kept on with the bed-making. We have a great many beds made, and next week will begin to give them to the Gregorian Armenians. We have just given out fifty beds to the Protestants, including pillows, mattresses, and covers. All beds are made substantially of wool, and will last several years. For cloth alone I spent £100 the past week. It is an immense work to partially clothe this people, now utterly ragged from wearing two months their one suit. I think I never was so glad to feel the spring-time approaching.

How to get work for the widows is my great problem. I turn it over in my mind early and late. Cotton work is the only thing I can see just now.

Mr. Sanders went to Garmoush (a village about an hour from here) last week. No massacre has occurred there, but the whole village is most wonderfully spiritually awakened. Gregorians come in large numbers, and are earnestly seeking light. There is quite a temperance movement in connection with these meetings.

March 6.

We have purchased cotton in the husk, and are giving it out for women and children to prepare by picking, cleaning, and spinning. Three hundred or more are now engaged in weaving, &c. We then use the cloth in bedding and garments. I am sitting now in our reception room with six women cutting garments.

March 11.

I have had a rare outing this P.M., *the first of my being in the street in four and a half months.* I have been to greet the wife of our new pasha just arrived. She is the Moslem I so much loved, and to whom in sorrow we ministered when she buried three daughters. She embraced and kissed me, and sat down by my side. When I tried to leave, they insisted on the pasha's coming in to meet me, and we five talked as freely as if elsewhere. All were so cordial and sensible, that I with redoubled assurance told the Christians on my return, they should no longer fear.

As our dining-room and kitchen each have a family, we use few dishes, temporarily on a shelf on my bookcase in my room, and eat from my study table, living on rations as served to the people about us, and two meals a day. I am physically in excellent state, but that accounts and letters keep me up too late after each full day of overseeing the dispensing of clothing and bedding. Some 300 to 500 are cut, tied up, and marked daily. We have a good investigating committee of eight or nine.

Money is at present coming in a degree to cheer us in our relief work, but it will be a long work, and friends must be patient in helping carry the burden.

What is to be done with the great mass of widows, probably over 1500, and some say 3000! All have children, without a father to support them—a bare house in place of former, at least comparative, comfort, and with nothing to wrap the new comers in. What wonder that some of the women in desperation expose their children to quick death, rather than awake the slow death of a future without means of support.

We are administering the relief in such a way as to enable as many as possible of the Christians to begin work. In those trades the produce of which can be used in relief work, the problem is easy, and quite a number of looms, which have been idle for a long time, are now running, and all the help given them is a small loan for buying thread. The product is taken by the relief funds at a very reasonable rate, and the weavers are put in a condition to support their families. We can use £200 or more a week for the next two months, and then only clothe a part of the needy.

We are now convinced that the loss of life here was 6000, and perhaps near 8000. The stench is yet very great in the Armenian church. There is a crack in the stonework of the gallery from which blood flowed.

We have this week opened a temporary home for convalescents. This course seemed imperative in order to save a few of our few men.

The church is packed every Sabbath to the very door. I never saw it thus before.

Yesterday in the midst of very busy cares, the mother of our High School teacher, who was killed, was announced. I was glad I did give time to see her though it upset me for a full hour after she and her companions had gone. The mother had lost her husband and two sons, her daughter had lost her husband, beside her father and two brothers, and a son of seventeen years. Her mother-in-law, a widow, had three sons killed and two sons-in-law. I could find no words, but could only weep. They evidently had no more tears to shed, were calm, but their sorrow had a depth which God grant few may ever know.

It is best for us to forget if we can.

April 1.

All party spirit between Protestants and Gregorians is a thing of the past.

After the massacre in ——, S.'s husband held prayer-meetings in his house, and large numbers attended, and many hearts were softened and turned to Christ. He continued this good work till in the last massacre he went to join the heavenly host of martyrs.]

LETTER No. XII.

VISIT TO THE BURNED CHURCH—A CALL UPON THE PASHA'S WIFE—
HER WARM SYMPATHY WITH THE SUFFERING PEOPLE, ETC.

OURFA, *May (probably near* 16*th*).

DEAR FRIENDS,—A day or two since Miss Shattuck, Mr. S., R. and I went to see the great church where the multitude, between 2000 and 3000, were killed at the time of the massacre, and an awful sight it was.

The two priests who remain alive (who were both wounded and left for dead), met us at the outer gate of the yard, and with very sad faces led us to their ruined church. As we entered, the first feeling was one, not so much of horror, as of awe and thankfulness to God, who has given such ability to man to confess to His name, and to suffer for His sake, and as we thought of the individual and collective victory of faith and faithfulness that was witnessed by Christ and the angels on that great day of the sacrifice of priests and teachers and people in this place, for the moment the greatness of the subject seemed to fill one's mind to the exclusion of anything else. Not that all the people massacred here were martyrs, of course; but so many were consciously and deliberately so, who *could* have escaped if they would have denied the faith, that their constancy casts a halo over the entire company who perished with them.

But these feelings gave place after awhile to the contemplation of the scene itself, and that in its turn to some slight imagination of the awful and unutterable agony that had been endured. Here is the enormous church—blackened from floor to roof—the roof, a mass of black, except where the white calcined stone shows through. All along both sides are the calcined and broken stone brackets which once supported the two great galleries where the women worshipped, and these galleries were crowded on that day as closely as it was possible. What must have been the scene as these fell in with their living burden upon the crowd, and into the flames below! There is another large gallery opposite the altar—not fallen—and from the crowd of women here, numbers of girls were selected and taken away to Moslem harems both here and at Aleppo. One sad tale I must tell, to bring home to your hearts the realisation which only detail affords, and then we will again reverently leave the Church and turn to other things.

One woman had sought refuge here with her husband and six children. She was a very nice-looking woman, and, in spite of her mature motherhood, still young, and a certain Turk had cast his eyes upon her. Her husband was killed in the churchyard; she saw it, and sought the church with her children; the Turk followed her triumphantly, saying, "Now I shall have you," &c. This drove the poor creature to despair, and she flung one[1] of her children into the flames from the gallery, and then exclaiming, "What is there to live for?" sprang after it herself and perished. The child was saved, and with four others of the family (for one was burned) will we hope be soon sent to Constantinople and taken under the kind care of Dr. and Mrs. D.

We learn that the people were lured to the church by soldiers going to their houses previously and telling them that if they went there they would be protected. One of the priests also told us that they knew who the chief instigator of this crime was, and that he sometimes meets him in the street, and when he does so, he, the Moslem, always smiles triumphantly at him!

I should have mentioned previously that the head priest, who was killed in the church during the massacre, having anticipated the fate which was hanging over the people and himself, had spent the entire night previously in administering the sacrament of the Lord's Supper, after the custom of their Church, to one after another of the congregation. Surely, whatever superstition may have mingled with this, to him, most solemn ceremonial, one cannot but greatly admire his devotion and constancy, and believe that it was accepted above as faithful service by Him whose eyes pierce earthly mists, and whose love accepts very imperfect offerings when truly offered.

You will remember that in a recent letter we spoke of a house kindly lent by an Armenian—who had had twenty-one of his family killed—for the use of orphans. When visiting it a few days since we were shown from the roof

---

[1] Query, *three*. *Cf.* p. 94.—J. R. H.

a cave under the wall of the city, which had been filled with bodies after the massacre, dragged thither by their heels, the cave's mouth being then stopped up with earth. While we were looking we noticed three or four Armenian women there weeping and wailing over the spot—no doubt their dearest were there buried!

Now for a change of scene.

On the 10th May I received intimation in the morning that at two in the afternoon the Pasha's lady would receive Miss Shattuck and myself. This Pasha, I think you know, is not the one under whom the massacre took place, but a really humane man sent to allay the excitement and quiet the people.

So, attended by our two guards and Miss Shattuck's man-servant, we went, and at the door poor Miss S. was in great distress because she had forgotten to tell me either to wear goloshes or to carry slippers, for no *boots* had ever before trodden those lovely carpets of the reception room! No notice was taken of my delinquency however, and I am sure I did not let one speck of dust fall upon the floor! The great lady and her son's wife—a very beautiful young woman, beautifully dressed and with her two little children by her side (quite a picture)—received us very graciously, and gave us the seat of honour, &c. The first half-hour was spent in polite nothings. One rug I greatly admired, representing the Eastern hemisphere in beautiful colours, on a crimson ground, which she said cost £90 or £100, I forget which, and so on. Then the young lady went out, returning with a tray on which were two elegant high silver-gilt vases with little forks in one, and in the centre a dish of preserved citron. You had to take a fork, spear a piece of citron and eat it from the fork, and then return the fork to the other receptacle, and this while the lady stands waiting. This ordeal over, a servant brought in coffee, and after that *real* conversation began.

I ventured, in spite of the many cautions I had received on the subject, to refer to the poor Armenian prisoners, and to say how we hoped and believed her husband would interpose on their behalf. She said he had already done what he could, though so far unsuccessfully, and would continue his efforts. None of us had dry eyes while we spoke of their sufferings and those of the people, and I then ventured to take the lady's hand while I said that the Christians of England would bless her and her husband if they would be like a father and mother to the poor Armenians here. She returned the pressure of my hand very warmly, and held it a while, saying, "It would be a heart of stone that would not be touched to think of what the Christian people had gone through." Both Miss S. and I believe her a genuine woman, and in her position she may do much good even within her harem walls. Other ladies (Turkish) called while we were there,—one the wife of a captain, who said that her husband had saved 200 Christians the day of the massacre by taking them into safe quarters. Of course I spoke very warmly in response. Before leaving we were both presented with pretty little bouquets—and these Turkish ladies are evidently fond of flowers, as they and the children all wore some on their heads.

The day following this visit (yesterday), imagine my

surprise to receive word that the Pasha's lady would return my call in the afternoon! I believe this unexpected celerity was to show *special* honour, though rather embarrassing to Miss S. and myself. I could not make many preparations except flowers, our quarters not allowing, and Miss S. discouraging my bringing our preserved ginger, figs, and raisins—of which I have a small store —in imitation of the citron, so I contented myself with coffee and half-a-dozen bouquets of roses.

R., our servants, and the guard had all to hide or be sent out of the house before the great lady arrived (Miss Shattuck bringing her from the Mission House, where she had previously called). She had four servants with her, and Miss S. brought a girl to hand the coffee, and as I watched them ascend our steps, each lady a bundle of black silk and gauze, I thought it a strange sight and very picturesque. They were most elegantly attired for indoors, however, when their wraps were removed, and I could hardly keep my eyes off the younger one, she was so exceedingly pretty (again with her little children about her). I had much feared beforehand that conversation would flag this visit, but it did not do so, as the elder lady propounded a scheme for bringing here a skilled worker in carpets from near Smyrna, and teaching the women to make them. Finally she promised to write to the most skilled whom she knew personally and make inquiries as to expense. They stayed nearly two hours, and nearly all the time one little slave-girl stood behind the young lady's chair, who was nicely dressed, and seemed very gentle, and had been bought at this same place—an Asia Minor

Sparta, I think. I suggested her sitting down two or three times to Miss S., but noticed that she did not think best to translate it. We parted from these friendly ladies with, I believe, very kindly feelings on both sides.

Our next letter will not exactly be ours, though a circular, but an abbreviation of a long letter R. and I have received from the Gregorians here about their church and schools.—Yours very truly,

H. B. H.

LETTER No. XIII.

A COMMUNICATION FROM SOME LEADING EDESSANS.

EDESSA, *April* 26, 1896.

DEAR PROFESSOR AND MRS. H.,—We respectfully welcome you to our obscure but historical city. Your presence here has been a great comfort to our afflicted hearts, and to the thousands of poor orphans and widows. We come to express our heartfelt thanks on behalf of the Armenian people of this city for your kind visit here.

Dear Sir and Lady, pardon us if we take this as an opportunity to present to you some concise information concerning this city—our birthplace—and concerning our Apostolical Church. Also concerning the events which have taken place in these "latter days" and the miserable condition to which our people have fallen, and concerning their vital needs, although we believe they are not unknown to your learned minds.

Ourfa or Edessa is one of the oldest of cities, and at the time that Christ did preach on earth it was governed by Abgar, an Armenian king of the dynasty of Arshazoony. This prince, who was contemporary to Christ, desired to know and hear about His teaching, and this desire he showed by sending messengers to the land. After the ascension of Christ, St. Thaddeus, one of the Apostles, came to Ourfa and preached the Gospel, both to the king and people, and founded the new religion. . . .

After the death of his pious father, the son of Abgar broke the legs of St. Adde, who was ordained as Bishop by St. Thaddeus, and afterwards put him to death, and his remains were interred in the same church, in a special sepulchre, where they continue till now—but the light of Christianity did not go out by this martyrdom. New disciples rose up, and although the Church of Edessa passed through many religious and political persecutions, from century to century, yet she remained faithful to her apostolical foundation.

In 1845 the Armenian bishop, Haretoon Kahengian of Edessa, considering that the remaining part of the temple was nearly destroyed, and that it was now holding a crowded congregation, began the building of a new and a larger church, which is now standing. . . . On this church the free labour of thousands of pious believers was spent. This mother church had about 20,000 children around her, who, having entered upon a path of mental and material progress, were expecting a very bright future; but alas! the year 1895 brought with it unexpected calamities which not only destroyed the flourishing present, but also ruined the hopeful future.

For the prosperous condition of the Armenians had excited passionate envy, and on October 25th the signal of the first attack was given to our Moslem countrymen by some armed men entering the Armenian quarter, and killing a harmless man, a money-changer, by name Baghas. On the following day violent attacks were made on all sides, and also hundreds of houses which were at the entrance of the Armenian quarter were pillaged. About sixty-five persons were killed and thousands of men, women, and children were taken by force to the barracks and there compelled to put on white turbans and to profess Islam to save their lives.

After these painful events the Armenians were besieged. They were deprived of water and victuals; besides this, about seventy Armenians were put in prison, on the pretext that they were revolutionists. After this the Government demanded all the weapons possessed by the Armenians for travelling purposes, on pain of terrible punishment as rebels, which they obediently yielded up, feeling assured that the Imperial Government would protect their lives.

On December 27th and 28th took place the second disturbance, in such a dreadful manner that we spare your feelings the relation of them in detail. It is enough to say that our Moslem countrymen plundered all our houses and shops, and fired very many, making an exception of such as were around the Protestant church, which were protected on account of Miss Shattuck, the American missionary, being a foreign subject. The Moslems carried on their deadly work by means of all kinds of instruments, *i.e.*, by Martini rifles, revolvers, bayonets, axes, daggers, spears, &c.; their aim was to kill all males above ten years of age. Many blind, dumb, sick, and crippled were among the killed.

Then the gendarmes advised the poor Armenians to take refuge in the church, because they said they were going to protect it. But, instead, the fiercest attack was made upon the church. They set it on fire, and men, women, and children, first embracing each other, were burned to death.

Many ladies and girls were dragged half-naked to the mosques, from which they were taken to different Moslem houses, according to the choice of their captors. After that, under threat of a third massacre, from five to six hundred weak Christians accepted Islam.

Without reckoning the wounded or those who have lost a limb or been paralysed through fear, the number of the slain is approximately as follows: 2350 men, 820 women, 1290 children. But it is thought that when all the names are collected the number will rise to 5000.

In deep sorrow we mention that among the slain there are found respectable, useful, and diligent public men.

Now this afflicted people, deprived of all its useful members, deprived of its rightful properties, is also deprived of the one single consolation which it can have on earth, namely, the Christian services which had their origin nineteen centuries ago. These have now for six months altogether ceased, on account of the injuries to the church. The capacity of the church of our Protestant brethren not being sufficient to hold the two congregations, many have been deprived of public religious comfort of any kind.

As with the church, so with our schools, which have been dispersed, and the poor forlorn orphans wander about in the streets begging. They are in great danger of being immoralised and turned to Moslems.

Thus the once flourishing congregation, which has never before held out its hands to others for help, is now in a languishing state. Those of them who have survived through the kind providence of God, are a group of poor men who, with their material goods, have lost all their means of livelihood; so much so, that they are utterly unable to rebuild the church and re-establish the schools.

Life in the last few months would have been unbearable if England and other Christian countries had not sent us material help through Miss Shattuck. These kind acts have made a great impression upon every heart of this poor people, and this sense will not easily pass away.

Now, dear Professor and Mrs. H., you that have left your happy land and on the wings of kindness have come as far as this unfortunate country, while passing through this half-deserted land you meet on your way a giant who is wounded. It is the people of the unfortunate Armenians. Alas! no surgeon passes this way Be good Samaritans to dress our wounds! And our needs are twofold. First, the salvation of souls, and morality of conduct; secondly, the rebuilding of our ruined church, and the establishment of an orphanage.

These two things alone will be able to comfort us and alleviate our indescribable affliction. These, if done, will keep together our thousands of orphans and widows in the bosom of Christianity.

Your manifest kindness permits us to apply to you in this righteous cause. But we are not sure that we are not infringing the laws of propriety when we request you to make an appeal to the celebrated generosity of the noble people of England, in order to the restoration of the church and the re-establishment of the school.

LETTER No. XIV.

SCHEMES OF RELIEF AND SOCIAL RECONSTRUCTION—ORPHANS,
WIDOWS, AND SCHOOLS.

OURFA, *May* 17, 1896.

DEAR FRIENDS,—I thought you would like to know that we are finding opportunities for helping the people here, in directly spiritual work, and in the matter of the prospects of this suffering people. This morning at 7 A.M. we had again a very large audience in the church; and I had the privilege of addressing them through an interpreter. At midday H. had a large company of women to talk to; not as large as at Aintab, but then Aintab is, relatively to Ourfa, a much more advanced place. It is no slight blessing to have an American college and hospital in a city; in Ourfa we have only a mission with schools.

After the morning service, we met by appointment three of the leading men of the community (Gregorian Armenians), in order to discuss with them the appeal which they recently sent us, of which you have a tolerably exact translation in our Circular Letter No. XIII. You will remember that they appealed for help in the matter of their orphans, their schools, and their ruined church. I had been thinking over these different points, in order to enter into right sympathy with them, as well as to form a correct judgment as to what was needed for the common salvation. The elementary needs of food, clothing, and shelter have, as you know, been met for the present, largely through the mutual helpfulness of the people, but with the supplement of the help given by the Westminster Committee, the Red Cross Society, &c. No relief, or next to none, has been given in money—a very wise restraint.

Postponing, then, the further consideration of beds and shoes and the like, we had to face the question of the readjustment of the social fabric. What was to be done with these wrecked and desolated families, often the mere shreds of once prosperous households? I told my Gregorian friends that the first thing to deal with was the need of the orphans, and that we had already, as they knew, made a start in that, and, as we could see our way, we would extend the work. But I pointed out to them that we were not building an orphanage in the European sense (which could not be done without firmans from Constantinople), but finding homes for the children for whom no homes were available (you will see from my previous message on this point at how low a figure we are able to work this maintenance of the orphans. Five pounds for a year is so moderate that a number of our friends might indulge in the luxury).

I then went on to the question of the widows, with the view of showing that this was a question, not of maintenance, but of finding occupations and industries. The women of Ourfa are not nearly as clever as those of Aintab; they have forgotten, moreover, an art which they once knew, of making embroideries in gold thread, &c. However, Miss Shattuck has been able to set them to embroidering felt mats in colours, and we have also made some efforts to revive the older kind of work, and expect some very pretty results. I cannot see that anything further can be done for the widows; we shall send specimens of their work to our friends for approbation, and with the hope of obtaining a market.

The next question was that of the schools; and this was very important, and demanded a long investigation. It may, perhaps, sound strange that we should lay stress on this point; but you will easily see that it is by superior intelligence that the Armenians have made such progress in the East, and it is imperative, unless they are to relapse into the old barbarism of fifty years back, that the schools be maintained and improved. The recent attack upon the Armenians was, if I may put it figuratively, a blow at the head. Most of the leading men are gone, and many of the teachers. And the recent calamities have made it impossible that the schools, which have just been reopened, can be at once self-supporting, as they were before the massacres. The Gregorians have reopened with about 300 children out of a former 500, and this they could not have done without the aid of the Protestants. The number of teachers is wholly inadequate, and there is no school for girls. There are thousands of children unprovided for. As to the Protestant part of the community, they lean somewhat upon the American Mission, and will recover more rapidly; they have begun work with 300 to 400 children, both boys and girls. The whole of the work is elementary in character, and there is urgent need for some provision of a more advanced nature.

On putting the thing into figures (with the fact before us that the Gregorian school building had not been destroyed at the time of the massacre, so that there was no question of buildings), I found that it was possible to provide accommodation for 400 boys and 300 girls, with a staff of ten teachers, six for the boys and four for the girls; and that these ten teachers could be obtained, in the present distress, for such moderate salaries as from 1000 to 1500 piastres for a school year of ten months; this sounds rather enigmatic, on account of the Turkish money, but it comes, *all told*, to about £80 Turkish, which is less than £80 English by several pounds. At this point I told them that I was prepared to furnish them with this sum for the first year, until peace should return and trade revive, &c.

But here I paused. We had still to remember that we were dealing only with the schools of the Gregorian Armenians; what of the Protestant part of the community? They were almost in as bad case, and we had to consider the whole question, and not a part of it. Moreover, we have been learning some of our old lessons about religious liberty and social progress over again in these days; and if we could put the education of Ourfa outside the range of religious jealousy and animosity, what a blessing it would be! So I proposed to our Gregorian friends the question, "What need was there for two separate committees to deal with the children?" Were they prepared to unite with the Protestants in a single committee, so as not to have any social friction, provided that they had a numerical preponderance on the committee in consideration of the fact that their school was the larger one. To my delight they replied at once that they had no wish to teach the peculiarities of their own church system in the school, and would gladly join with the Protestants in the formation of a School Committee, if it should be found that the Protestants wished it. And I promised in that case to furnish them with £120 (Turkish) for the first year for the joint-committee. The question of one or two higher teachers we hope to be able to deal with later on.

I feel pretty sure that this is the right thing to do. The Armenian holds his own here, because he is brighter and better educated than the rest of the community. Recent events have put him down at the bottom of the ladder; and as the Armenians say in their appeal, the children are "immoralising" in the streets. Unless they are rescued, many will be far behind their dead fathers and mothers, and some of them will be in danger of a change of religion. It seems to me that the rescue of the children intellectually is as important as shoes for their feet, or beds to sleep on.

From this question we passed to a much more difficult one, viz., the restoration of the great church, which was the scene of so many martyrdoms. The Armenians at present are conducting a little service in their school, where about 600 people meet, the rest of them worshipping with the Protestants. Their great church holds several thousands, but its interior is ruined, and the fabric has been declared unsafe by the Government. The pillars are calcined by fire, and perhaps part of the roof also. They estimate that it will take £2000 to restore it, and want help to do so. I was obliged to tell them that I did not at present see any way of making this appeal public, because the Sultan was hardly likely to permit them to rebuild with foreign money. If they could obtain permission to worship within the blackened walls, I urged them to do so; but this they said was prohibited by the authorities. As I did not see what steps to take to help them, we agreed to defer the matter for the present. One naturally feels no slight interest in the repair of a building which has become historical in the Christian world; and they have no other church in which to worship. But what could one say or do in such a case? And now I must conclude my little report.—Sincerely yours, J. R. H.

Postscripts by H. B. H.

. . . I have much sympathy with the two forlorn priests and the few leaders of the people left who mourn over their ruined temple, and who pray continually for its restoration (yet it does not seem as if the money entrusted to us should any of it go to such a fund).

R.'s meeting this morning and mine at noon with the dear women were very interesting times. After my meeting the women all stayed to kiss our hands, Miss S.'s and mine, filing up one aisle and down another, several hundred, and most of them with tears in their eyes or running down their cheeks. Some *would* stay to tell of husbands and children killed; but there were so many, we (Miss S. and

I) had to pass them on when we would gladly have listened. I spoke from "Let their widows trust in Me."

Miss S. is a truly wonderful woman, and so free from self-life; but oh, she is so tired! and there is no possible release, not even for a day. We had planned a three days' excursion to the "Haran" of Scripture, and had all arranged to start to-morrow, but now word comes that the Pasha cannot permit or give guards, as he does not consider it safe. There is also a very pleasant gentleman, a missionary, here for a few days, who travels around; they both come in to our quarters for a little fellowship every evening.

Our next journey will be to Mardin; but letters must go still to us, c/o Bible House, British Post-Office, Constantinople. You cannot think how much we want to hear. We have had *no letters at all* since leaving Constantinople, April 9.

The heat is commencing here. We are both fairly well.

P.S. (20th).—Since writing, letters of April 29th have come and greatly cheered our hearts.

Everything here is at a standstill, except the spirit of inquiry about spiritual things, which is awakening among the suffering people, and which is really wonderful, and a prophecy to me of good things to come!

Our plans are changed, as the Pasha says it is not safe for us to go to Mardin now, the road being frequented by wild Arabs, so we are going, *D.V.*, to Diarbekir next Monday instead.

LETTER No. XV.

OUR FOURTH SUNDAY IN OURFA — WOMEN'S MEETING IN THE PROTESTANT CHURCH—AN ARMENIAN BETROTHAL—LETTERS FROM MISSIONARIES.

OURFA, *May* 24, 1896.

MY DEAR FRIENDS,—This is our fourth Sunday here, and I am just home from the morning meeting, which began about 7 A.M. I had the opportunity of speaking again through an interpreter, and such an attentive audience! We shall not easily forget the privileges which the Lord is giving us in the way of ministering to this suffering people, and you may imagine our heart-strings are getting tangled up with them by this time. It brings us into unexpectedly primitive Christianity to be standing in the place of a martyred pastor and to be preaching to an audience of confessors, where many bear the marks of deep wounds, and all have lost a heavy percentage of their friends. And such a patient people! I never hear any resentment from them, only desires for peace, and, if possible, for escape from the net in which they are caught.

Now we are moving further east, and expect to find even more acute suffering and worse physical distress than here, if one may judge by the letters that reach us from those quarters. Our next stopping-place will be Diarbekir, and after that we go to Mardin, where we have a most cordial welcome from our friends at the American Mission. How long this will take we cannot tell yet, and beyond that we have made no definite plans; indeed, all our plans are made subject to the revision of the pillar of cloud by day and the pillar of fire by night.

I enclose two letters [1] from missionaries in the district to which we are now moving, which will give you an idea of our prospects. If any public use is made of them, it will be best not to quote names of places and people more than is necessary for intelligence.—With remembrance to all our people, sincerely yours,

J. R. H.

Postscript by H. B. H.

You may like to know that last Sunday I had the privilege of holding another women's meeting in the Protestant Church, Miss Shattuck interpreting. The large proportion of these dear veiled and sheeted creatures were widows from the massacre, and all had lost dear ones. It was a most interesting sight—perhaps eight hundred or more—of whom a large proportion stayed to kiss our hands, and some to tell their tales, very briefly of course. I longed to put all *your* love and sympathy as well as my own into my words, for I felt it a beautiful "opportunity" given by God for endeavouring to cheer and comfort. I spoke from Jer. xlix. 11.

On Saturday we attended a very different gathering, the first one of a genial kind that has taken place among the Christians here since the massacre. It was the be-

---

[1] See p. 92.

trothal of the daughter of the murdered Protestant pastor, a sweet young girl who has acted as a mother to her little brothers and sisters since that time, to one of the Relief Committee, a Mr. Koradgian (whose uncle is now in England), and belonging to a very nice family.

Miss Shattuck had the party at the mission-house, and R. and I had special invitations from both her and the bridegroom's family. We felt it right to go, and were very glad afterwards that we had done so. The dear people seemed so pleased, indeed R. told them if they made any more polite speeches about our presence we should think it was he and I who were to be betrothed afresh! About fifty guests were present, and the women (I cannot call them ladies, it sounds so conventional and European) were in semi-bridal costume, with flowers in their hair or on their veils—for all the married ones were veiled even in-doors.

Before the religious ceremony began R. was asked to "make a few remarks," which, rather reluctantly, as it was so unexpected a request, he did, and then there were other little speeches. The bride-elect was by no means conspicuous either in dress or place in the room, and the bridegroom did not even look her way as he came in, but, followed by a crowd of men friends, went to another part of the room entirely and took his seat.

Lemonade (or a drink like it made of some flower) was served first, and when all had had and drunk a large glassful, Mr. Sanders, the American travelling missionary, performed a little ceremony of prayer, Scripture-reading, and singing. Then the bridegroom took a beautifully bound Bible and hymn-book (from Constantinople), wrapped in a blue and green silk scarf, and presented it very bashfully to the young girl, who, never once looking up, took it and gave it to Miss Shattuck to put back on the table again, and then they exchanged rings, also with the same shamefacedness; and then both retired to their places once more, not a word having passed between them.

After this the bridegroom-elect's sister, attended by a maid, carried sweetmeats around, giving two bundles to the highly favoured and one to the less so. As I received my two the first, I made the mistake of saying one would do for R. and me together, but found I was quite "out" as to etiquette, and our four bundles now adorn our room!

Then Miss Shattuck gave coffee all round, and after this the ceremonious part of the affair was over, and conversation became general, I mean between the men friends and the foreigners, for the Armenian women never talk except when quite alone, and then they *do!*

Several young girls were present whose betrothed had been killed, but for the time the sadness was lessened—I could not say it was all gone, for every speech referred to it—but one could see how capable of pure, true enjoyment these people are, who have been called upon to drink a cup of such almost unparalleled sorrow. Before the friends left I felt as if I must express to the bridegroom and his father my prayer that he and his wife-elect might live to see the deliverance of their people.

After the betrothal, no matter how long delayed the wedding may be, the etiquette is that the young man does not visit at the young girl's home.

Letters from Mardin.

May 10, 1896.

MY DEAR PROFESSOR H.,—Your favour of the 3rd inst. was received to-day, and was quite a surprise to us. We heartily congratulate you and Mrs. H. upon your successful journey thus far. The mail of last week informed us that you were *en route*, but we had not supposed you were quite so near us. May the dear Lord prosper you and yours everywhere you may go in this part of the country. We have long been longing to see you, and to do for you all we possibly can to put you in the way of attaining the objects of your visit. As to hints for your guidance, I scarcely know what to offer, as I do not know just what line you are desirous to pursue. Can't you come on here first direct from Ourfa, and then perhaps Brother D. and I can help you to lay out your plans with reference to the best times to be at this place and that, and the order of your itinerary, with perhaps fresh information about this, that, and the other place. For instance, I can give you a letter of introduction to the Jacobite Syrian Patriarch now residing in Diarbekir. We are on a pleasant footing with him.

We are still busy with relief work, and in the last two days, Friday and Saturday, we aided over 1500 souls to money, comfortables, and felt mats, to serve in lieu of mattresses. Day after to-morrow we send off L.T.100 (*i.e.*, L.T., pounds Turkish) to the monastery of Mar Kriârkos, in the Beshare Kuzze, north of the Tigris, and in a few days a second distribution at Nisibin. The Sanjak and Aliân will take between £300 and £400, some 3000 being on our lists from that region alone. There are between 25,000 and 35,000 needy souls, hungry, poorly clad, and with almost no bedding in the district we are trying to look after, though for more than a month now the Government has succeeded in stopping our work in the Redwan and Sert districts through the arrest and imprisonment of our distributing agent. We were stopped twenty days here on all kinds of relief work, and a month on *industrial* relief, though now we are again in full blast, the Government having backed down from its domineering attitude.

Were it not for this relief work I should be tempted to go on to Ourfa to meet and escort you to our Mardin home, but I have thrown everything else aside to push this business day and night, while D.

runs the station and the school work. Mrs. A. joins me in Christian love and greeting to Mrs. H. and yourself, as also to Miss Shattuck.
—As ever, cordially yours, A. N. A.

[*N.B.*—These missionaries are evidently caring for a very large district. Nisibin is about fifty miles from Mardin; Redwan, sixty miles; Sert, eighty miles, &c.—R. H. F.]

May 12, 1896.

DEAR MISS SHATTUCK,—You have been much in our thoughts these past weeks, and I should have written you but for the uncertainty whether or not you are in Ourfa. We hope you are *kept* in health and peace. What an inexhaustible mine of comfort and encouragement we have in the Word that is *sure* and *tried!*

We are so glad Mr. Sanders has been with you—perhaps he is still —if so, our greetings to him. We are all in reasonable health and strength, though Mrs. B. is a little indisposed this morning; nothing very serious, I think. How good God is to keep us all so well, and give us strength for the extra burdens. Our hearts are sick and sore at the prospect—we see nothing to encourage or give hope save as we lift our eyes above to the everlasting hills of refuge and help— *they* are always there, for our help cometh from the Lord which made heaven and earth.

Mr. A. gives all his time and strength to the relief work, which taxes them to the utmost. I should say that he also supplies Pastor Jurjise's pulpit at the Sunday morning service while he (pastor) is in prison.

Relief work was stopped for some days, but has now started up again. The destitution and want are beyond all description. Last week Mr. A. and I made a hasty visit to one of the near villages that was destroyed between 500 and 600 houses—a most pitiable sight, the ruined houses. The building was of *karpeetch*, I suppose you know that word, the sun-dried brick covered with poles and earth; many of the walls were broken through or partially thrown over,— the large poles had generally been carried away, though in some cases the whole roof would seem to have been burned, that is, the combustible part of it. A few wretched families were gathered in the two stone churches—Syrian Jacobite and Syrian Catholic—as the Government insists on their returning to their village. Remembering what a busy hive of industry the place was in former years, the present desertedness, with the listless, apathetic air of the families found, seemed to me inexpressibly sad. On our way home we made a little computation of the material damage wrought; it seemed to us that £500,000 was a low estimate! But the demoralisation among the survivors, the *moral* damage, in what terms can it be estimated? The brightness and beauty of spring seems almost a mockery, yet we *know* that God is good, and His mercy endureth for ever.

I purposed a word of sympathy and cheer, but I fear I have missed it. Your experiences have been so much harder and sadder than ours.

Mrs. B. sends you her warmest love.—Very sincerely yours,

N. C. D.

[I add the following interesting letter from Ourfa.—J. R. H.]

Letter from Ourfa.

May 18, 1896.

MY DEAR MISS M.,—You will be interested in the following story of the six orphans we are to send to Mrs. D. of Constantinople. The oldest is fourteen years and the youngest ten. Their names are Hagop, Armen, and the twins—Victoria and Ozmo—and Zexapat. Their father was a merchant. All his goods were stolen, and he was wounded in many places on Saturday, December 28, in his home. He lived that day and night. The next day, when the massacre began again, though suffering terribly, he started with his wife and children for the Armenian church. He died in the street. His body was left in a house near. When the church was attacked the mother and children were in the church, on the second floor. Turks came up the stairs after killing many on the first floor. The grandmother of the children took Hagop and Victoria and got down the stairs, Turks seized Hagop and were about to kill him, when a Kurd took him and said he wanted to keep him, but after three days sent him away. One of the Turks said to the mother, "We killed your husband yesterday because I wanted to marry you." Both the mother and children tried to get away from the Turks, but finding they could not, decided they would jump into the fire which had been started in the church. This poor mother threw down Armen, a boy of eight years, and Ozmo and Zexapat, and then she leaped down after them. The mother and the boy of eight years were burned, but though the others were burned some, and considerably harmed by the fall, they are now well. We send with these our pastor's son of about six years, as Mrs. D. said they would take six children.

I am too weary to do best work, and hope to get refreshment in a trip to Haran, taking me away from home three days. Mr. Sanders urges me to go with Professor H. and wife, and we expect to start in the morning. I enjoy Professor and Mrs. H. every minute I can be with them. You can scarce know how pressed I am, yet usually I am *peaceful*—so kept by the prayers of my friends and trust in God for each moment. I visited the interior of the Armenian church last Saturday for the first time since the change. I did not, after all I had heard, believe it what I saw it to be. It made me nearly ill for that day. It is terrible, beyond all language to describe the testimony that the pile gives to the *agonies* of the occupants. Well that you are not here. You could not endure the strain.

May 19*th*.—During the past week we have been collecting the children for Smyrna and Constantinople. Yesterday, on making application to the Government for proper papers allowing a quiet and undisturbed journey, the Pasha said, "No, *we shall attend to the orphans ourselves.*" (It now seems a settled plan of the Moslems to get these girls into their harems.) It is hopeless for us to try to do anything more. I am wondering now if these children will be left undisturbed in the temporary home we have opened here in Ourfa. I am so sad that I cannot write more of it now.

The Pasha says it is unsafe for us to go to Haran, and so we must not go. Many and constant and continued thanks to you for your efforts for funds. We need it all.—Yours affectionately,

C. SHATTUCK.

[I add a farewell message which I received from some of my Armenian friends in Ourfa, omitting the Armenian text, and giving their own English translation.—J. R. H.

OURFA, *June* 1, 1896.

To Rev. (*sic!*) Professor HARRIS.

DEAR SIR,—Your condescension to visit our city, the kindness and the sympathy which you have shown to our afflicted brethren, have filled our hearts with deep gratitude. Indeed we are at a loss how to express our feelings, especially for the great help you have done for our orphanage and the schools. We cannot but admire your noble heart. We ask your pardon for our own inability to express our gratitude personally when you were here, and by forwarding to you this proof of our feelings we implore the Almighty God to bless you, and send from on high His heavenly rewards of more enduring.]

LETTER No. XVI.

WE LEAVE OURFA AND VISIT GARMOUSH AND SEVEREK—A NIGHT IN A HOVEL—MASSACRE IN SEVEREK—OUR SERVANT CLAPPED IN PRISON — A NIGHT IN A KURDISH TENT — ARRIVAL AT DIARBEKIR.

DIARBEKIR, *June* 1, 1896.

DEAR FRIENDS,—We left the much-beloved Ourfa and dear Miss Shattuck on Tuesday, May 26th, the latter kindly accompanying us some miles on our journey on her plump little mule. Mr. Sanders had left a few hours earlier for Aintab, so after speeding us on our way, this brave woman returned back with her servant and guard to her lonely home and work, and to the special effort of endeavouring to obtain leave, once refused, to send her little prepared band of orphans to Smyrna.

Our first night was at Garmoush, the Christian village of which I wrote you in my last, which had been so miraculously saved by a storm, so that the marauders and the Moslems had themselves said, "Allah does not will it"—*i.e.*, the destruction of the village. Here we stayed at the house of a Protestant pastor, and here we found to our regret that a very fine old Armenian copy of the Gospels, for which R. had offered a good sum, and hoped to get, had been plastered up again inside a wall, fears having prevailed, and was therefore lost to him and scholarship.

After a long day's ride the following day, during which we saw many locusts, a plague of which is threatened, we stopped at a Kurd village, the like of which may none of you ever be called upon to enter!

The mud hovel in which we did *not* sleep was occupied by a crowd of villagers, our two *zaptiehs*, a number of muleteers, our two servants, and ourselves, besides the closest proximity of dogs, horses, and mules. None of these companions could, however, vie for a moment as to disagreeability with the fleas, each one as big as four or five English ones, which left us not a moment's rest, while a heavy thunderstorm rolling overhead towards morning completed the chaos.

We started before it cleared next day, and reached Severek about 6 P.M. I got soaked to the skin with the storm, though R. happily had his waterproof, and neither of us were the worse, as the hot sun, when it did come out, soon dried my clothes. At Severek we went straight to the little Protestant church and pastor, and slept the night in the school-house.

This town has suffered very terribly, and there are many hundreds of widows, and they have had *hardly any help*. We therefore have promised to get some sent there, as the people are "all hungry, all needing clothing and bedding." We also left a small sum. The pastor, Abraham Haratunyan, is an extremely earnest young man, a graduate of one of the American Mission colleges, who was simply teacher previous to the murder of the pastor; but he seems to have had the prophet's mantle descend upon him, as his preaching attracts not only

G

Protestant and Gregorian *people* (as at Aintab and Ourfa), but the Gregorian and Syrian priests also, who say to him, " We wish to hear you whenever you preach."

This good man is one of those who braved death for Christ's sake. He was offered the usual choice, "Islam or death?" and chose death; so they cut him about and left him for dead, but he afterwards revived and is now well. He and another confessor who had had two guns held to his breast, and expected death instantly, but something intervened, told us, on my asking if they felt no fear in the prospect, "*No fear*, for we expected we should directly be with Jesus, but the flesh trembled a little." This was said so simply that it struck me much.

We had scarcely had time to sit down, much less to change our riding clothes, when our visitors began to come; and soon we had a room full, and had quite a reception—the Syrian "Metropolitan of the East," the Gregorian priest—the *one* doctor from whom all his medicines and appliances were taken at the time of the massacre, so that he could do nothing for the sick and wounded, and who looked the most forlorn and helpless doctor I have ever seen—a fine old Armenian gentleman once *very* rich, from whom everything had been taken, and others. R. and I sat at one end of the room, the Metropolitan at my side, a very fine old priest, and the rest all in front, and for a long long time they told us of their sorrows, and of one woe after another.

Close behind us on the wall were thick blood and brain stains, where the previous Protestant pastor had been killed by an axe-blow on the head, smashing in the skull and scattering the brains. Right up to the ceiling were these blood-marks, and all around, from a clearly-marked centre to a wide diameter. So under the blood of his martyrdom we conversed, with those who had been equally confessors of Christ, though their lives had been spared, of the past and future of their nation, and of the realities of the faith we held in common, endeavouring to cheer them with the hope that however much man had failed them, God was even now working out some grand design of love for them. R. quoted to them that couplet of Trench[1] beginning—

"Though the mills of God grind slowly, yet they grind exceeding small,"

and they all caught at the idea in a moment, and seemed to feed upon it.

We had hardly parted from these most interesting guests before a very different party entered, viz., the Turkish *kaimakam*, or governor, and his officials and soldiers—also quite a company. They were very gruff and not at all friendly, though the great man *did* condescend to drink our coffee; and he put R. through a very long and unpleasant cross-examination, and also had our two servants in, and treated them the same way. How thankful we were that our previous visitors had

---

[1] *Not* Trench, though at first sight it has the appearance of being from the "Century of Couplets." As usually quoted in English, it is Longfellow's translation of a German couplet, which itself goes back into a verse of a lost Greek poet, which is quoted in the Sibylline Oracles, in Sextus Empiricus, in Origen against Celsus, and furnishes a text for Plutarch in his famous tract on the Tardy Vengeance of the Deity.—J. R. H.

departed when these arrived, as it would have been very dangerous for them to have been found with us.

This cross-questioning elicited the fact that our poor Alexander had no passport (in fact, there is no doubt in our minds but that he is with us because he has escaped from his own city of Aleppo, but concerning this we have asked no questions). Imagine our grief when, after thinking we had passed through our ordeal safely, the following morning he was sent for and put in prison! Poor Griva, the cook, was in despair, and the boy had behaved so beautifully and devotedly to us throughout our travels that we felt as deeply concerned as if a real personal friend were in trouble.

So, as Bunyan says of his pilgrims, we "betook ourselves to prayer;" and after awhile R. obtained permission to call on the *kaimakam* on his behalf, the Protestant pastor, who speaks English nicely, accompanying him to interpret. I sent a special salaam and request in my own name, and after R. had explained and mollified the great man, the pastor proffered my petition, and the reply was, "Well, in consideration of your wishes, and for the sake of madam's petition, I will forgive him." Thus our prayers were answered, and we received the boy back again with great rejoicing.

All danger for Alexander is not over yet, however, as R. was obliged to promise to report him at Diarbekir, and the Pasha here is very severe indeed, and the one under whom all the atrocities were perpetrated; but after so signal a deliverance we are not inclined to doubt final success, and my great desire is, after our journey is over, to send Alexander to Robert or Aintab College, for he is extremely quick and intelligent, and if educated will make a very useful man, I think.[1]

Of our journey from Severek to Diarbekir, the chief feature was one night in a Kurdish tent. We did not want to go to the Kurds at all, but it was a choice between that and the open hillside on a chilly night, and without proper appliances, and our chief *zaptich* was determined we should go to the tent. Indeed, he pretty nearly pulled me off my horse in his energetic demonstrations, and we thought it wiser to surrender.

These Kurdish tents are not at all like the elegant ones travellers are accustomed to in Palestine, but huge goat-hair sheets of canvas stretched on poles, and not touching the ground by four or five feet, divided by reed fences about four feet high. Alexander soon spread our rugs and pillows in a corner, and barricaded us in with our luggage, and the chief and his wife came and smoked the pipe of peace, and gave us milk and *kaimak* (sour curd).

So we resigned ourselves to circumstances, but it was the wildest scene we were ever in. The wild Kurds— men, women, and children—came and stared at us in party after party, but offered us no rudeness, and we were as friendly as looks and smiles and biscuits could go; and so after awhile the excitement of our coming subsided, and all resumed its ordinary course. Just the other side of the reeds by my side two camel foals were

---

[1] The young man escaped from Constantinople at the time of the August massacres, and has reached England in safety, where he has found a place of service.—J. R. H.

lying down, while the mother of one of them kept invading the tent, and being as often driven out. The soldiers and Kurdish men were sitting over a wood fire close by, smoking and talking in that peculiarly high and unpleasant key I shall never forget, which is habitual to them, and almost amounts to a scream, and always suggests anger; while on the other side the women and children prepared their mats for sleeping, and our servants kept watch and ward. I did not think under such circumstances that either of us would close our eyes, but we were very weary, and by-and-by the scene all faded away, and the next thing I knew was the grey of early morning, and our men were preparing for the start. So without food or drink we mounted about 4.30, and pursued our onward course.

On the second day from this we reached Diarbekir (yesterday), and have ever since been hearing fresh horrors, past and present, from Mr. Hallward's dragoman and his wife—Mr. H., the British Vice-Consul, being away—and a young Armenian doctor who studied in Baltimore, and who is nearly wild with indignation, pity, and fear for the future of his people.

All these beg and entreat us to do something to help the people to emigrate. "If we have to leave our houses, our property that was, everything, we will go all of us, so that only our lives are granted us." The dragoman says that almost the entire population of Diarbekir would emigrate if the way were made, for otherwise they will die of starvation next winter.—Affectionately,

H. B. H.

LETTER No. XVII.

DIFFICULTIES AT DIARBEKIR — A ROUGH RIDE TO MARDIN — EXCURSION IN SEARCH OF MSS. — ALEXANDER IN TROUBLE AGAIN.

MARDIN, *June* 15, 1896.

DEAR FRIENDS,—We left Diarbekir on Wednesday, June 3rd, under some difficulty, my having taken some photographs the day before of the walls of the city and of a ruined Christian village across the Tigris, coupled with some incautious remarks of one of our servants, being the immediate occasion, but behind that, no doubt, a strong Government suspicion of strangers. Again and again, when we thought we were off, was the consular dragoman summoned to the Government headquarters to answer some fresh question about us, and at last, after we had been put under guard of a centurion and two inferior soldiers, and had started to walk to our *arabas* or springless waggons outside the city, which had been awaiting us for a couple of hours, we were stopped, and had all to go back again and undergo fresh examination.

You can imagine our pleasure, then, when we really found ourselves outside the city gates, and this time riding inside our carriage instead of upon horseback, and actually by the side of the Tigris! But whatever our pleasure was in escaping from Diarbekir, the term is hardly applicable to any other part of our ride to Mardin, and many a time did we repent of having quitted the saddle and its evils to "fly to others that we knew not of."

A large part of the carriage road (so called) between Diarbekir and Mardin is no better than a rough river-bed with boulders, the small ones as big and bigger than one's head, over which it is one series of bumps and jumps, until one wonders that one's neck is not dislocated. The floor of our *araba* was spread with our bed-coverlets and our pillows piled at the back, but they made no appreciable difference as to the result; and then the night in the sheikh's house!—but I will not attempt to describe what those who travel in this country in summer suffer at night from fleas, though you must know that sleep is out of the question except in brief snatches. I hope we shall soon sleep on the roofs of our resting-places instead of under them, as the natives mostly do in summer.

Our escort swelled to nine soldiers before we reached Mardin next day—a fact due probably to the desire of these poor men for a little proper food, since they left us on our arrival here without asking any backsheesh (a quite unusual event). One of them, a Kurd, flourished a lance —instead of bearing gun and sword like the others—fully fourteen feet long, and when galloping about with some of the others (for our edification from time to time) he looked just like a picture.

Mardin, which we reached in two days, is in a mountainous region, most picturesquely situated, with a wonderful old castle on the summit of a grand rampart of rock overlooking the city. All around the country was desolated last autumn and winter by Kurds, though more by pillage than actual massacre, and hundreds of villages were laid waste. The consequence is that here is one of the large Relief centres receiving help from the Duke of Westminster's Fund, and not less than 20,000 to 25,000 people have been at one time receiving help, and about 15,000 are now being regularly assisted. This work will soon be closed for the summer.

Mr. Andrus, one of the missionaries here, is the head of the Relief Committee, and has done a splendid work. He is at it morning, noon, and night, having handed most of his missionary work over to his colleague, Mr. Dewey, but though his energy seems boundless and his resources and devices for helping the sufferers endless, yet one can gather from word and look that he with all the other missionaries whom we have met look at the approaching winter with great uncertainty and dread.

The population of the devastated region referred to have next to no harvest, and what they have is even now being eaten by the Kurds' camels, horses, cattle, and sheep, which they are pasturing with great triumph on the Christians' corn; and what can be done? Of course this is not everywhere—a request for sickles came in yesterday from one district—but it is very general.

The refugees here have been put to road-making and mending in the neighbourhood by the Relief Committee (not the Diarbekir road, alas!), but the money will only do a very little in this direction; and what then?

This city was saved from massacre by one very powerful Kurdish family or tribe, which lives here, who, though thieves themselves, are friendly with the missionaries, and for their sakes saved the Christians of the city. Mrs. Dewey told me that from the elevation of the mission premises they could see the plains around black with the Kurds day after day, who were gathered together for the purpose of massacre and only waited permission. This however they did not get, and had to retire again. For in no place did the Kurds dare to kill without express permission.

This mission centre is not Armenian but Syrian, and one notices a decided difference in the character of the people. They do not seem to me nearly so intelligent and refined as the Armenians, but we are told they are more trustworthy and less fickle, but have had no opportunity of judging of this ourselves. Also one notices far less spiritual awakening, far smaller audiences in the church, and less interest. This may arise from the fact that massacre was averted here, and that they have not had the baptism of blood and fire of other places to drive them to God—I cannot tell—but the difference is very manifest in spite of the beautiful and continuous work and effort of the faithful little missionary band here, equal, I suppose, in earnestness to that of any other centre.

Now I must tell you that R., accompanied by Mr. Andrus and helpers, has gone out on a little tour in the neighbourhood, manuscript-hunting. This is a special centre for Syrian MSS., and many which are of great value are known to exist in the neighbouring monasteries and churches. But the priests also know their value in one sense very well (though not how to utilise this value), and they will not sell. All they seem willing to do is to lend a book for a short time, and this is of course very tantalising to R. However, perhaps this trip may be specially successful; we are hoping that it may. It will be a very fatiguing one at any rate, and I shall be thankful when it is over, which may not be for two or even three weeks.

I did not go, as there would have been no special object, and I am quite settling in to the life here and enjoying it, and finding also little bits of work to do. Our one recreation, after the day's heat and work, is riding, and as the missionaries have really beautiful animals, and are fearless riders, and they kindly provide me with a good mount, we often go out for a run, which is very different to ordinary travel, and quite a change.

Our Armenian boy got himself (and nearly the community) into grave trouble a few days after his arrival here. He went out at night, as at Ourfa, to try and get some of the dreadful dogs around shut up. This was specially on my behalf, as he knew how they annoyed me; but in dealing with a neighbouring dog, he forgot it was a Kurdish and not an Armenian one, as at Ourfa, and was threatened with being killed by its master, and the next day, in the bazaar, he was attacked and badly cut on the head, hand, and arms, and beaten as well, the Moslem soldiers standing by and not interfering. When I saw him after he had been rescued, he was a sorry sight, the blood all streaming from his head. His injuries were not serious, however, and we administered quite as much admonition as sympathy to him afterwards; and it is now understood that in Kurdistan the dogs are to be left alone.

Our friends here are finishing their present school term in a few days, and having examination. I am attending the English examination only. When this is over they close up their work for a time and retire to a country home about two miles off.

Before concluding this letter, I should say that the native Protestant pastor here is in prison and under sentence for five years, and his only crime—that a copy of a scheme of reforms was found in the possession of another person, who said that the pastor had given it to him! He is said to be a very good man indeed. When we return to Diarbekir we will hear from the Consul whether there is any hope of a reprieve, though, being a Turkish subject, of course Mr. Hallward can do nothing officially for his rescue.—Your friend affectionately,

HELEN B. H.

LETTER No. XVIII.

CLOSING OF THE HIGH SCHOOL—IMPOSING CEREMONIES—
VISIT TO THE JACOBITE SCHOOLS, ETC.

MARDIN, *June* 22, 1896.

DEAR FRIENDS,—Life here is very quiet, while R. and Mr. Andrus are away on their manuscript-hunting tour, the one great event being the closing of the Missionary Schools (High Schools) for the summer. These schools have not been interrupted as those at the other missionary stations have been, there having (as I before mentioned) been no massacre here, though all the country around was pillaged, and one burnt village lies in its desolation on the plain just below the town. The examinations had been going on for the previous week, but as it was all conducted in Arabic I did not attend, except the examinations in English, which were creditable, if not brilliant. But early in the morning of Wednesday, June 17, I went by special invitation[1] to witness the recitations and diploma-giving—first in the girls' school, under the superintendence of Mrs. Andrus, and later in the boys' department, under Mr. Dewey.

These schools are not large, the boys numbering only forty-five and the girls twenty-five, but being High Schools

[1] I was the first European visitor they ever had.

they mean a constant supply of good education for the elect of the young people of the town and neighbourhood. Imagine us then in the bright and airy (though heavy) stone building of the girls' school-room. The windows are prettily draped and adorned with flowering geraniums, &c., though their strong iron grating (common to all windows in the houses here), prison-like, reminds one that danger abounds even during the most peaceful times and occupations. A large part of the room is devoted to the use of the relations of the girls, and here *great* interest is manifested—the women, veiled and in native costume, occupying one part, and the men (an American innovation) another.

The graduating class were all neatly dressed, and had flowers and ribbons after the manner of girls generally, while one, richer than the rest, added necklace and bracelets to these. Their part was each to read a composition of their own to the assembled company, which they did with as much modesty and yet self-possession as English girls could have shown. Their subjects were —(1) The advantages of learning for women. (2) The love of one's country. (3) By what means can you lift yourself to a higher plane of life? The boys' declamations were on similar subjects, viz.—(1) Civilisation. (2) Your relation to your country. (3) Perseverance in well-doing. (4) Fight the good fight of faith.

With the boys (or young men, for I suppose they were eighteen to twenty years of age) declamation was the object, the subjects being selected, and truly these young Syrians did *so well*, with hand and eye, as well as voice, that I could not but tell them afterwards I thought they were not behind the students I had heard give their commencement orations at Haverford College, U.S.A., some years since. This, of course, pleased them *immensely*, as America is their beau-ideal in all things. But I felt I must go further still, not this time in compliment, but in the earnest expression of my desire that their education, as well as natural powers, might be dedicated to the service of God, and, if it were His will, to the preaching of the Gospel to *their own people*. The two eldest boys at once responded *most earnestly*, with uplifted hand and eye, according to the Eastern habit, and the words, "May God grant it!" and "If He permits it!"

On Friday I had the pleasure of visiting very different schools, namely, those belonging to the ancient Jacobite Church. This, you know, is the oldest Church in this part of the country, and different from the Gregorian or Armenian, which is probably its contemporary. It is much purer in faith and practice than the Syrian Catholic, which exists here also, and much less bigoted. When taking us over the adjoining church, and showing us the pictures in it, the teacher and sexton took care to inform us that *they did not worship them*, they "were not so ignorant as that;" but at the same time, I must own they showed some superstition by bringing us "a piece of the true Cross," and some bones of saints, as very precious treasures!

In the boys' school, the little fellows, all with the red fez on their heads and their legs tucked under them, spouted for us several of their dirge-like Church hymns, and then the teacher asked me if I would like to ask them some questions. This surprised me much, not only because I was a Protestant, but also a woman. However, being pleased with the liberality the invitation showed, I responded and asked what they could tell me about Bethlehem, the Message to the Shepherds, &c., telling them a little of our visit there. To my great pleasure, the boys answered quite as well as they would have done in any English school, and then at a word from their teacher, changing their position to a kneeling one, they sang an Eastern Christmas carol for us—very well indeed. All these young Syrians were perfectly grave and well-behaved during our visit, and all rose to their feet, both at our coming and going. I have given this incident somewhat at length, to show the friendly relations between the American missionaries (for it was a lady missionary who took me) and the ancient Church.

Yesterday (Sunday) the Protestant service was at 6 A.M., and a native gentleman preached. At 2.30 I had a meeting for women, though much smaller than at Ourfa or Aintab, because there is not at all the same spiritual awakening here as in those places; and afterwards there was a "Christian Endeavour" meeting and a boys' school.

The post (weekly), to which we look forward so much, has just come in, but brought us no letters, alas! I wonder where they are, for I feel sure some of you, dear friends, have written to cheer us up with news from "a far and beloved country" within the past month. Well, we must wait, and have long patience, for many things (letters included) while in this unhappy land, and in due time, no doubt, there will be a reaping time, if we faint not.—With love to all, your friend sincerely,

HELEN B. H.

LETTER No. XIX.

FIRST RUMOURS OF THE VAN MASSACRE.

MARDIN, *June* 29, 1896.

MY DEAR FRIENDS,—I have very little personal news for you to-day, for our life here has gone on very evenly since I last wrote; but the rumours that are coming in are most disquieting. We have no certain news except a telegram from Dr. Raynolds of Van to the effect that the missionaries are safe, but the rumour in the market-place here is that every Christian at Van has been killed, and that the Government have turned the cannon on the towns of Erzeroum and Bitlis and levelled them with the ground.[1] There is a great panic here, of course, and the Christian men who have any money say they will take out their papers and go to Beyrout, or anywhere, and leave everything. We hear also of Arab risings near here, and altogether it seems as if a new reign of terror is commencing.

R. and Mr. Andrus have not yet returned, but we expect them to-morrow, and probably at the end of the week we shall return to Diarbekir (which is, however, in a most unsettled condition). Our future movements we

---

[1] The state of things at Van was not quite so bad as the alarmist rumours painted it, though the outlook was dark and sad indeed. And the other reports as to Erzeroum, &c., were not substantiated.

must leave entirely to that Divine guidance which has been so wonderfully with us hitherto, and believe that in some way God will use our presence here for His own glory. He keeps our hearts and minds in His own peace.—Yours affectionately,

HELEN B. H.

P.S.—We have received large budgets of letters from the Bible House and from Aintab, and are grateful. Miss G. Kimball is returning from Van to America, for which I am very sorry.

Excuse so poor a letter. I had a nice meeting with the women yesterday (Sunday), in spite of great heat. The missionaries here are most kind, and we have much fellowship with them every way. Their one thought is for the people.

LETTER No. XX.

A MODERN SIMEON STYLITES—BRIEF ACCOUNT OF A VISIT TO THE TÛR ABDÎN—VISIT TO A TURKISH PRISON, ETC.

MARDIN, *July* 3, 1896.

DEAR FRIENDS, — In visiting among the Christian women to-day I have just heard a very interesting history of one of the men martyred at Harpoot during the massacres, and must send it on.

He was originally a Jacobite monk, and from a boy of fourteen he sought by penance and self-inflicted suffering to buy the forgiveness of his sins. After his conversion to Protestantism he showed his adopted mother (who has just told us about him) the scars all round his body where he had worn a belt with nails in it, and when Mr. Andrus found him first he was in an old disused cistern in a small monastery near Midyat, in which he had fastened a rope from side to side, and when sleep came on he flung himself across it to keep himself awake to pray. In fact he acted as like St. Simeon Stylites as a modern monk could. Before this, however, and when he was first *en route* with other lads for the monastic life, an earnest native preacher had met him and prophesied to him that he should yet see the insufficiency of the way he had chosen to walk in, and would leave it and believe the pure Gospel.

Mr. Andrus was the instrument through whom God opened his eyes, though Bibles had previously been introduced into the monastery, and this young monk with others was earnestly reading for himself; when he once saw his errors he, with the same earnestness and determination which had marked his monkish life, renounced it, and took a theological course at the Protestant college, and had just gone through it and was ready for ordination when the end came. He was one of those martyred as well as massacred, and tortured as well as martyred. His adopted mother showed us his photograph, and told of his name written in the family Bible with those of her own children, and then with a sob added, "When they asked him to deny Christ and he refused, they cut off one of his arms, and then said, 'Will you not become a Moslem now?' 'No,' he replied, 'for I have come to this hour in God's will and appointment, and I will not change.' Then they literally cut him to pieces before finally killing him." The photo shows a face of no ordinary force of character, and especially of great determination. His name was Baulus Bursom or Paul Barsauma.

H. B. H.

My dear Friends,—I do not know that there is very much of special interest to report. The greater part of the last three weeks has been spent by me in the mountains to the north and east of Mardin, as far as the Tigris river. This is the Mount Masius of the ancients, but in the present day is known as the Tûr Abdîn, or Mountain of the Servants; I suppose it acquired this name from the frequency of the monasteries which are found all over the district. By a mixture of Syriac and Arabic it is often called the Jebel Tûr, which is a mere repetition (Mt. Mountain). A dreary country enough, for the most part bare limestone crags with a little growth of scrub oak, and almost waterless in many parts, except where the limestone gives place to some more generous soil. The interest of this country to me lies chiefly in the fact that the Syriac language is still spoken here, both by the clergy and the people, and there is hardly a church where there are not some Syriac MSS. It is a good district also for studying the decline and prophesying the approaching decease of Syrian monasticism, for most of the monasteries are either in ruins or so much reduced as not to be much better than ruins. I am glad to be at the bedside of this erratic religion, and if a shake would hasten the patient's dissolution, I would gladly give him a brace of shakes.

It is also a good country for studying the decline of the Turkish Government; for the people are almost bled to death by their unjust rulers, and I found village after village either wholly deserted or reduced to a fraction of its original population, while the hill-sides were full of traces of ancient vineyards, and fruit-trees were growing wild that must at one time have been carefully cultivated. There has been no systematic massacre over this region, only habitual oppression and local outbreaks of disorder. We passed through one village which had been raided a few hours before by Moslems, who had carried off 300 sheep; but these robberies ought hardly to be classed with what has been going on in other places, for they are probably as natural to the life of the people as the ancient Border raids between England and Scotland. However that may be, the decline of the prosperity of the district was to me very patent, and one can only hope that the sick man who is responsible for the state of affairs will before long find some one to give him also a necessary and sufficient shake.

The travelling was very hard and rough, the more so because the hot weather has now fairly set in; so that although there was generally a favourable breeze, and we were seldom at a lower altitude than 4000 feet, I found my endurance well tested. We had often to rise very early in the view of a hard day's riding; the last two days were especially heavy; we were up on these two days at 1.40 and 1.30 A.M., and in the saddle at 2.50 and 2.40, riding six hours at a stretch before we had a proper breakfast. But the night air and the early morning air are wonderfully refreshing, and I do not find any unpleasant result except a little extra weariness, which will soon pass off.

As to the results of this little expedition, well, they were a little disappointing; a great deal of damage had been done in some places by the Kurds, who have an especial spite against books, and love to show their antipathy to Christianity by destroying the Gospels. One monastery where we hoped to find interesting matter was completely ruined, and all the books destroyed. It is fortunate that we do not live by books alone. In other places the people had walled up or hidden away their treasures, or if they showed them, resolutely refused to part with them. So you will easily see how disappointments can come in battalions.

To-day (July 3) I have had the opportunity of visiting the Turkish prison in Mardin in company with my friends of the American Mission, Dr. Andrus and Mr. Dewey. We went to see the Protestant pastor and teacher, who have been for more than seven months in prison on the charge of sedition and treason. You will be surprised when I tell you what it all amounts to; a copy of reforms supposed to be those agreed upon by the European Powers (though I suspect the whole document was a forgery) was found in the possession of the teacher, and it was maintained that he had obtained them from the minister. A charge of treason was laid against them both, and they were sentenced for a term of years. Happily we hear that there is some chance of a new trial being granted in consequence of appeals made to Constantinople, but what the outcome will be is still uncertain.[1] You can put this case along with the rest of the Turkish caricatures of justice, such as the case of the preacher who was condemned for having a copy of Lord Salisbury's speech in his pocket, &c.

We were not allowed to go into the wards of the prison, but only into an outside room, into which the prisoners were presently brought. I should have liked to go over the whole of the building, but all I could see was a courtyard with a tank in it, a number of men sitting in the shade under one of the walls, and at the tank a man

[1] Unfortunately the sentence was confirmed.

helping another prisoner, who was heavily ironed, to wash his face, a new version of the law of bearing one another's burdens.

We had a pleasant interview with our incarcerated friends, who seem to be well cared for. An Eastern prison is not like one of ours. The prisoners feed themselves, except for a ration of bread and water supplied by the Government, and this means a certain amount of access to them from outside. They were bright and cheerful, had books, I think, with which their friends had supplied them, and, on the whole, my first impression of a Turkish prison was favourable. If we are to be thrown into prison on frivolous charges, it is something to have one's books and one's dinner sent to one from the outside.

And now our time at Mardin is coming to an end, and we move northward. We hear good reports of the work done by our Red Cross friends in the district to the east of Harpoot; one of them, Mr. Wood, is not many days from us; he was at Diarbekir till the 25th of last month, and is now organising relief at Meiafarkin, a place not far to the north of Diarbekir, where there seems to have been much suffering. Apparently we have just missed seeing him, but perhaps we may meet by-and-by.

With best wishes to all our good friends in England, sincerely yours,

J. R. H.

[*Note.*—Miss Kimball writes to the Women's Fund from Van down to 22nd July. She expected to start for England 4th August. The results of the late outbreak were not yet known; entire regions, in which terrible things had happened, were still shut up by the Kurds, but it was evident that the whole province was utterly laid waste. About 6000 were still on their relief bread list in the town, on the principle of just keeping soul and body together, but they were trying to reserve funds for the yet darker times of autumn and winter. Help, after Miss Kimball leaves, is to be administered conjointly by the British Consul and Dr. Raynolds, the solitary representative remaining of the American Mission. They still continue the four bakeries at a total cost of £45 per week. The Government severely refuses all applications for permission to emigrate or leave the town.—R. H. F.

Note.—For reasons which belong to secret crafts, as well as because such fox-hunting as I was engaged in does not properly belong to the Armenian question, I have not in this place told all that I know about the diffusion of Syriac literature in the Tûr Abdîn. There is, further, no law requiring one to dilate upon one's disappointments. One thing at least was the reverse of disappointing, the bath in one of the rivers of Paradise, the loving remembrance of which induces me to add a fragment of a private letter to a brother who has often partaken of such aquatic joys with me: "MIDYAT, *June* 21, 1896.— . . . How many times I have wanted thee lately. But most of all this last week, when I was washing away the accumulated sin of a week's travel by bathing in that sweet river of Paradise whose name is Hiddekel, Diklath, or Tigris. If thou hadst been there and under the same burden of the flesh and that live and dead matter that clings thereto, how sportively would we have swum across it, at the risk of landing a quarter of a mile lower down, to say nothing of being indited by the River Conservancy Board of Mosul under an Act to Prevent the Pollution of Rivers. We might even have conspired to do, what I ached after, we might have hired a *kellik* or raft on skins and floated down. It would have only cost us five days to Nineveh, and we could have been better than Hemerobaptists, of whom the Sabean remnant exists down the river at Bagdad. But wishes are of small service, and the axiom 'I wished for Leonard there' does not verify itself with 'I found him in Llanberis.'. . .

I am taking a week or two to search this mountain (Mount Masius) for some early relics which ought to be extant amongst a people who talk Syriac to you and understand you when you talk back. It has been hard work some of the time. If we have not exactly been 'bedmate of the burdock and the snake,' we have been under the sign of the Scorpion, and have our own interpretation of 'fighting with beasts at Ephesus' . . .

One day this week we were up at 3.30 and in the saddle at 4 (breakfastless), and did not reach our sleeping place till 7 P.M. By the end of that day we came to a country where there was no need to prohibit the use of opiates.

My love with this. Goodness and mercy are following us as though they belonged to our caravan. 'Sister' is in Mardin, busied with good works and orisons in which we are both remembered."—J. R. H.]

LETTER No. XXI.

JOURNEY FROM MARDIN TO DIARBEKIR—FORDING THE TIGRIS RIVER—INCIDENT AT A DESOLATED VILLAGE—NATURE AND EFFECTS OF THE MASSACRE AT DIARBEKIR—THE FRENCH CONSUL—PLANS FOR FUTURE MOVEMENTS.

DIARBEKIR, *July* 9, 1896.

DEAR FRIENDS,—Having purchased two very nice horses for ourselves at Mardin (for the sum of about £16 for both), we had a much less fatiguing return journey to Diarbekir, sixty miles, than the *araba* ride thither. We were accompanied part way on our first day's journey by the two gentlemen of the mission, Mr. Andrus and Mr. Dewey, and also the two younger ladies, Miss Pratt and Miss Graf, and we have become so attached to the brave little company who hold the fort at Mardin that it was not very easy saying good-bye, especially as we left them surrounded by so many difficulties and dangers. The night before leaving we had, however, a very comforting season of united prayer, and we are sure that we left them as truly safe under the shadow of the Divine wings in their lonely station, as that we ourselves are led and guarded in our going forth once more.

We were quite a cavalcade in this setting out, and more numerous than we wished, by the customary addition of soldiers. Four of these, with the Chief of Police, were appointed to accompany us; so with five military, four missionaries, two servants and a muleteer, and a Syrian Christian gentleman who attached himself to our party, and ourselves, we were fifteen in all, and when all were on the canter together it was quite a pretty sight looking back. Indeed, one time the soldiers became quite excited, and, quitting the beaten path, galloped round and round on the hillside, flourishing their guns at arm's length in the left hand, while the Chief of Police (by no means either a young man or light weight) went along with the rest, whirling his sword over his head, and all five shouting *à haute voix*.

This man has anything but a satisfactory record with regard to the late troubles, but having no choice as to having his company or not, we did our best to be kind to him, giving him portions of Mrs. Dewey's nice American cookery at each meal, and in return he always had his own carpet spread for us, sitting on the rocks or ground himself, and when I thanked him was profuse in his declarations that he was the one under obligation, and so on. Thus we reached our journey's end quite friendly, regretting that with so kindly a disposition he should at the same time have been so frightfully cruel when acting under the direction of a fanatical religion and Government.

We forded the Tigris before entering Diarbekir, to cut off a bend in the road, and as the current ran with great force and it was a good width, it was something of an undertaking. Of course we got pretty wet, and to add to my trials my horse lay down and rolled on the dry soft

sand the moment we landed, and I had only just time to
extricate myself from the saddle. It was extremely hot,
however, and we soon dried up, and came into Diarbekir
at the Mardin Gate in excellent spirits.

I should say that after crossing the Tigris we passed
through a desolated village, by name Kahby. Somehow
I did not at the first moment understand what the silence
and desolation meant. We had forgotten, in the pleasure
of nearing our journey's end, that we were surrounded by
the marks of the havoc of last winter, and when we passed
one large building after another (for these houses are built
like granaries or fortifications, very high and solid, and
quite different from those of the southern plains) with no
sign of life, and all more or less dilapidated, it seemed at
first as if we had fallen upon some recently excavated city
of the past, and then, in a moment of course, the real
state of the case rushed into the mind. Of the one
hundred houses belonging to this village, the Consular
Report gives eighty as having been burned!

As we were leaving it, a poor Christian woman suddenly
appeared from behind a building where, no doubt, she
had hidden on our approach, and seeing a lady among
the party, rushed up to me and took my extended hand
with gesticulations more eloquent than words. It was
sad to leave her with only the small expression of
sympathy I was able to give by a warm hand-clasp,
but delay was not possible at the time. I wonder
what her tale would have been could we have stayed
to listen!

We received a very kind welcome from our consul, Mr.

Hallward, and later on from M. Meyrier, the French consul, who dined with us.

I am sorry to say that this delightful gentleman is soon to leave Diarbekir, but my regrets are not on his account, for he has had a truly awful time here, and has not dared to leave his responsible post even to visit Mardin, since he came two years since, but I lament for the people whom he has so helped. He was alone here at the time of the massacre, for Mr. Hallward did not come till afterwards, and he was the means of saving fifteen hundred lives at the risk of his own and family's safety, by opening the Consulate buildings to the Armenians. He also made efforts which restrained in some degree the tide of diabolical cruelty, and stopped the massacre after three days, through the French Ambassador's remonstrance with the Porte. His wife and four children were with him in the Consulate, and for three days they could not be screened from sights and sounds the most terrible. He has since sent them to Constantinople.

Even here, however, the Moslems were not equally fanatical, and M. Meyrier told us last night, when we dined with him, that on one of these massacre evenings, believing himself to be alone, he threw himself on his divan, and gave way to a burst of uncontrollable weeping. Suddenly four or five Moslems made their way into the room, but he could not at once restrain himself, and continued weeping, while covering his face from them as much as was possible. Seeing this, they all sat down in silence at first, and then one after another broke down and wept too (and he said they were real tears!). Explain the phenomenon as we may, the fact is, at any rate, some alleviation to the general tale of horror.

We find things in a terrible state here. The two consuls are not able to grapple with the needed work, and cannot, of course, do anything among the women like the lady missionaries, and the distress is dreadful. Three Christian Protestant women called on me to-day and told me such horrors, and they say there is no one in Diarbekir who has not lost some near relative, husband, or father, or brother, or wife, while the sufferings of the poor abducted women and girls are beyond words. About forty of these have been reclaimed from neighbouring Kurds, and before leaving Diarbekir I am going to make some arrangement for helping them, for, of course, they are perfectly destitute, besides being utterly brokenhearted.

I had arranged to visit a good many of the Armenian women in their own houses, and so to hear their tales with my own ears, but we are so entirely under supervision that this very plan was immediately reported to the authorities. The women are now afraid to be brought under Government notice, and so I have given up the idea, but shall have opportunities on Sunday of speaking both to the Gregorians and Protestant women after their usual services, and of reading my letter.

R. has had a good deal of disappointment here on the manuscript question. The Syrian Patriarch who controls all the MSS. of his Church is said by our consul to be a man of very bad character, in league with, and in fact a nominee of, the Vali here who carried out the massacre.

Whether from our known friendship with the American missionaries or from the simple fact that ignorance and fanaticism hate Western scholarship, the fact is that he has set himself to prevent R. seeing the books he most wished to see, and told the Vali, while we were at Mardin, that *he should not let him see them!* This is very trying, but we comfort ourselves in the thought that the issue of this matter not being in our hands, but under Divine control, we may leave the matter where it is without fretting about it, R. having done all that has seemed possible to obtain access to these treasures (which undoubtedly exist, and may be, we trust, reserved for some future more successful investigator).

We are going to Harpoot on Monday (the 13th), and expect to stay there a while till we shall have time to hear from England. We were planning to omit Bitlis and Van from our route, partly because of recent events, and the apparent uselessness of expecting to find more valuable MSS. in the present state of panic in these parts, and also because every one here, and the two consuls the most recently, are anxious for us to do all in our power to promote a speedy Government permission for emigration, for which it looks as if our presence in Constantinople to make representations to the authorities, and especially *the Ambassadors there*, would be a necessary part.

But yesterday we received an urgent appeal from Mr. Atkin, of the Duke of Westminster's Committee, to remain here for some months longer, we being presumably the only English travellers in this part of the country, and, since the Red Cross agents are now recalled to Constantinople, the only persons with permission to go from place to place, which lays upon us great responsibility.

Will you aid us in our decision by sending us your united and individual judgment on this matter, for we do not see clearly for ourselves? Tell us also what the Friends' Appeal has brought forth, and how we stand as regards funds to administer. Probably we shall leave £100 or £200 for the destitute women here, and our little fund is getting low. Please send our letters still to Mr. Peet, Bible House, Constantinople, as we communicate with him by telegraph.—Yours affectionately,

H. B. H.

LETTER No. XXII.

I

ATTEMPTS AT RELIEF IN DIARBEKIR AND NEIGHBOURHOOD — A REVIEW OF HAMIDIYEH CAVALRY, ETC. — A SAD LETTER FROM AINTAB.

HARPOOT, *July* 18, 1896.

DEAR FRIENDS,—You may remember that in my last letter I spoke of a poor Christian woman who had rushed up to me from behind a wall at the ruined village of Khayad on the banks of the Tigris, as we were coming from Mardin, and with whom I had clasped hands for a moment. She had also made a similar appeal to R., and we thought little of it at the time; but afterwards, when we found that if the village were repaired *the people could return to work and quiet life,* and that there was no special money at Mr. Hallward's command for this purpose, we felt that we had had through that silent appeal a special call to the work, and so left £100 with Mr. Hallward for the purpose of rebuilding it, and the same sum for another still more utterly devastated village, or rather small town, called Kitabel, also on the Tigris, close to Diarbekir, where very many were killed, and witnessed a good profession for Christ, especially the Protestant pastor.

We have also felt it right to leave the same sum for

the relief of the utterly destitute women with whom this city abounds. The wife of Mr. Hallward's dragoman and another Christian woman, both graduates of the American College at Harpoot, have undertaken the investigation of cases for us, and they will send their reports to the Consul, who will advance to them according to need. This help is, of course, only to carry the poor creatures through the present distress, and does not deal with the future, for there is *no industry* for them to turn to here as at Aintab and Ourfa, and no lady missionaries to organise anything of the kind. Many of these helpless and needy ones were once wealthy ladies who had their own servants, and lived in every (Eastern) comfort; now, with husbands and sons killed, and their homes entirely pillaged, what can they do? When I asked Madame Tomas, the dragoman's wife, "What can the poor creatures do?" she replied, "There is nothing they can do, only they look to God, for He only can help."

Then, besides these, there are the poor ruined village girls who have been brought back, after months of imprisonment worse than death, from Kurdish homes, recovered at last by the indefatigable efforts of the French and English Consuls. There are many of these now in Diarbekir who have no homes and no parents to return to, and whose moral nature as well as physical health is all crushed and broken with what they have gone through. Again, what is to be done with them? I have told my small committee to try and find them *some* work—*anything* to occupy their minds—and to feed and clothe them.

Then there are the maimed and the sick! One poor young woman was brought for me to see, both of whose hands had been literally cut to pieces while endeavouring to save her head, which was also wounded, during the massacre, her husband being killed at the same time, and she, poor wretch, after his death and her own mutilation, bore twins (just think of it!), but, from being unable to nurse them, the babes of course died—a matter of much grief to herself and other pitying women, though to me it seemed more cause for thankfulness than sorrow; and yet what a tragedy! This woman, I need not say, is on our list.

I made an effort to get a large woman's meeting here as elsewhere, and the Armenian bishop had given leave, and planned for it in the great church at the close of the early Sunday service, when soldiers from the Government came "making inquiries," so it was relinquished, and also the plan for R. to speak in the Protestant church at the same time. Afterwards, however, I met, and read my letter to and addressed about fifty women in the dragoman's house, where his good wife holds a little prayer-meeting every Sunday, and the letter was listened to as always with many tears.

Although thus prevented from ourselves taking any public work in Diarbekir, we were cordially invited to the native Gregorian service, and given places of honour on the chancel platform of the great national church, all the people rising, both as we entered and retired, to show their appreciation of our visit of sympathy to their suffering town. And how they have suffered here! Three thousand massacred at once, and all the Christian shops and numbers of houses burned and pulled down!

You see, there being no mission station at Diarbekir nor relief committee, there has been little heard in England of the sufferings here. The French Consul, of whom I have already written, has done his uttermost most nobly, and since he came, Mr. Hallward, the British Vice-Consul, has spared no pains to investigate and help, and has been sustained by the Relief Committee at Constantinople; but all that has been done has been but as a drop in an ocean, and our contribution will also only help a very little; and yet it is a comfort to know that every little relieves *some* of the misery, and lifts *some* of the weight of despair from the hearts of the helpless and almost hopeless. Could permission for emigration be once obtained from headquarters, probably a very large number from Diarbekir would be among the first to go.

You will think it strange if I now tell you, as I think I must, one incident of our stay in this place—an incident which almost made one wonder at one's own identity, and yet probably it was permitted to give us an insight into the inner life of the oppressing race and of the wild people under their command.

One afternoon, as I was sitting on Mr. H.'s balcony quietly reading one of Dr. Westcott's works, the dragoman came in great haste to know if I would ride out with the Ferik Pasha (the Turkish military commander) and the two Consuls, as well as my husband. I naturally thought it was to visit some neighbouring scene of interest, and of course complied, feeling that we ought to do everything in our power to be friendly with the man who has so much control over the destinies of the poor people here, and who has shown himself far more merciful than the Vali, although the head of the military. Imagine, then, my feelings when I was escorted to a large tent outside the gates, and with R. and the Consuls given the places of honour, with Turkish officers and soldiers all around, and a display of the horsemanship of the Kurdish cavalry as our entertainment!

Whether this was devised to impress us as English people with their skill and warlike prowess, or was in regular order, and we only invited from courtesy, I do not know; but it was a scene of barbaric interest and wonder, *impossible to describe.* The beauty and pace of the horses, the skill and enthusiasm of the riders, the shouts, the gesticulations and cries of the soldiers, the waving and brandishing of lances and swords baffles description, and yet the control of the whole fantasia by those in authority—horseman over horse, and commander over commanded—was perfect.

It did not last long, such a show could not, and after coffee and hand-shaking, and as few words as possible, we returned and had a long discussion on the peace question afterwards with the Consuls—the Frenchman of course thinking our hopes and anticipations for the future coming of the kingdom of Christ, of peace and goodwill on the earth, quite impossible and Utopian. On the other hand, all we see and hear of the evils of national hatred and fanaticism only convinces us more than ever of the necessity and certainty that all this must pass away, and

this and all other countries become at last subject to the
Prince of Peace.

One thing is cheering us even now amidst the gloom, and
it is that permission has been given for those who have,
under fear of death, or more generally under fear of the
dishonour of wives and daughters, professed Moslemism,
to return to the Christian profession of faith, and numbers are availing themselves of this privilege and are so
doing. At Biredjik, for example, where there was not a
single professed Christian when we came through, 120
have now returned to the faith,[1] and have asked for a
Protestant pastor to be sent them, and so also in other
parts. This is cheering, and the accounts we still receive
of the advancing tide of real conversion and faith in
Aintab, in spite of much trouble there, is also very cheering and encouraging in regard to other places where we
believe the same change will soon take place; but we
will let our Aintab friends speak for themselves, and so
enclose a letter from Mrs. Dr. Fuller just received.—Your
friend affectionately,

Helen B. H.

II.

Mrs. Dr. Fuller to H. B. H.

Aintab, *July* 4, 1896.

My Dear Mrs. Harris,—Your very kind letters of
June 5th and 15th are at hand. I have been quite
poorly of late, or the Ourfa letter would have been answered

---

[1] A result which was due to the energy of Vice-Consul Fitzmaurice.

at once. Our hearty thanks for the efforts you and your dear husband are making in the emigration scheme. Your loving labours have already born fruit. Last week we had letters from Miss Frances Willard and from Mrs. Amos, both writing hopefully of the matter. We have replied at once and have assured them of our most earnest co-operation in any plan to ameliorate this distressed, dying nation. Now very little aid is coming to us. Starvation stares them in the face, and we have a horrible winter in prospect. Oh, is there no merciful hand to save these perishing ones? Now is the time to strike for it. Let there once be a beginning, the rest comes easier. We are writing everywhere on this subject. . . .

All our circle are quite well, though much worn from the strain. College commencement passed off very quietly, only a few friends of the graduates present. In place of flags there were flowers and mottoes. Seventeen graduated. Many of our youth are fleeing to America. Who wonders? I had a good letter from our student Baron Abraham of Severek, who spoke with great warmth of your visit there, and of your kindness. He is one of our most worthy young men, and we felt it to be a calamity to the college, when he was obliged to stay out one year to teach. He is a junior. His high Christian character has been the means of helping many of his companions in the college, and of leading some to Christ. He writes of his work and hopes. God spared him for some great purpose. He was my teacher in Armenian, so I thoroughly know him, and thoroughly trust him.

The weather is very hot here, and takes all the little

strength I have quite away. The Governor will not guarantee our safety at the mountain, only five hours away, even with a guard, so we are prisoners here. There is nothing to do but to keep as cool as possible, both in body and in mind. We are having many applications from the Gregorian community for college next year, but alas we are so crippled I fear many must be turned away, and we may not be able to keep all our professors, which will be a great calamity. We hope we can tide over this year in some way, but the outlook is very dark. If the friends at home could only realise our sore straits more fully! Never did we need support more. We *must have it somehow*. There is a marvellous awakening here. Many from the Gregorians are inquiring the way to eternal life. Visitors are appointed to go from house to house for prayer and reading of God's Word. The services are union on the Sabbath and on week-days. The Sunday-schools also. Over 1500 in the Gregorian Church (of children). Truly a nation may be born in a day. The harvest is ripe, but the labourers how few! Our pastors are all worn out with the demands upon them. Deeply spiritual laymen are helping also, yet the force is weak. Miss Shattuck wishes some one for Ourfa. What shall we do? We have tried for five weeks to get a helper there.

Mr. Fuller joins me in warm love for yourself and Mr. H. The Lord be with thee and bless thee.—Yours in Christian love, my dear Mrs. H.,

A. G. FULLER.

III.

Private Letter from H. B. H.

HARPOOT, *July* 21, 1896.

MY DEAR FRIEND,—The *Friend* with report of the Yearly Meeting is now to hand. We think that our Ourfa letters about the orphanage there, and Miss Shattuck's subsequent letters which I have forwarded, will have indicated to the committee one *very clear and plain way of immediate and beautiful help*, and perhaps also they will assist in the schools, which have already succeeded so wonderfully. We have advanced enough money for the current year for both—and are answerable for four years more for the orphans—and if Friends accept this burden it will leave us more to disburse for some of the innumerable pressing needs all around. Will you let us know *as soon as possible* where we stand in this matter—as we shall be very glad indeed of more ready money for the hungry, and needy, and houseless people about us. Could you not telegraph to what extent we may count on Friends for the immediate pressing needs of the people? Of course emigration is the one present hope for the people, besides keeping them alive. If it is not in some way carried out this autumn, multitudes *must perish*. Every one (consuls included, and of course missionaries) says so. The mass of destitute humanity is so great, *some must be lifted off the rest* in this way, or very few will be able to do what they else could to recuperate. They will crush one another. What makes Ourfa so much better able to make a fresh start than other places is no doubt that so many were killed outright, and those who are left have a chance to do something.

Here, the massacre was small, but every one suffered, and hundreds of villages were pillaged and their houses burned; and although a great deal has been done for them, and some 60,000 people kept alive, yet they have no means of livelihood, and no homes for next winter.

Our Red Cross friends, of whose work we hear such good accounts, have now left this country, and God's blessing will, we are sure, follow them. They laboured largely in this field, but they had not enough funds at their disposal (wisely as they administered them) to do more than help the people for the immediate distress.

The food-relief work is now closing for the summer, and our missionary friends dread the scene, when they shall tell the people they have no more bread for them next week. The people will then be thrown back on mulberries and a kind of wild spinach that they dry— for they cannot possibly afford *leben*[1]—or the sour curd which, with bread, used to be their chief sustenance. Now that we have appeared on the scene every one is looking to us, yet we have only what is left of private friends' gifts, and have not as yet had any of what Friends have publicly raised. Thus you will, I am sure, sympathise with our position, and relieve it as soon as possible.

[1] Turkish: *yaghoort*. *Leben* is the Arabic name.

Our address is still as before, and letters reach here better from Constantinople than from Aintab or Ourfa.

HELEN B. H.

P.S.—Just as I was closing this, a note from the Consul arrived, telling of a telegram from Constantinople announcing the receipt by Mr. Whittall of £1000 for Professor H. We are deeply and profoundly grateful for its receipt just at this time, and please express our special thanks for its extreme appropriateness.

H. B. H.

LETTER No. XXIII.

JOURNEY FROM DIARBEKIR TO HARPOOT—TAURUS MOUNTAINS—SOURCE OF THE TIGRIS—HEROIC BAND OF MISSIONARIES AT HARPOOT: STORY OF THEIR PRESERVATION DURING THE MASSACRE AND IN THE PRESENCE OF DEATH.

HARPOOT, *July* 22, 1896.

DEAR FRIENDS,—We left Diarbekir for Harpoot early on the morning of July 13, accompanied for the first hour or so of our journey by our kind friend and host, Mr. Hallward. Towards evening we began our ascent of the Taurus mountains, and all the following day were in their midst, now climbing up, up, up; and then winding down again through some narrow pass or beside the edge of some steep precipice, while all around the wild and lonely mountain scenery every moment seemed to offer some fresh beauty or wonder to our view.

We kept very near the Tigris a good part of the way, and at one part it was extremely beautiful, rushing over a rocky bed with great volume and force. We believed we finally traced its source to a wonderful blue lake of "incredible crystal," as Mr. Ruskin would say, which lies high up amid the mountains, lonely and without even a boat on its surface, reminding us very much of the Sea of Galilee (except that it is smaller), and our imaginations, looking forward to the good time coming when this country shall be open to civilisation, pictured it a lovely summer resort for the dwellers on the neighbouring plains, all dotted over with white sails, and its shores with happy homes.

Our descent on the third day into the great plain on the northern side of the Taurus was very tedious and trying, especially as we accomplished it under a blazing sun —but our good horses never once made a false step—and before evening we had arrived at the Government village Mezreh, at the foot of the steep hill of 1000 feet high, on the summit of which Harpoot stands, and were met and kindly greeted by our Consul, Mr. Fontana, and also by Dr. Barnum and Mr. Ellis, two of the missionaries from Harpoot, who, after we had stayed a little while in conversation with the Consul (who lives at Mezreh), escorted us up the hill to their fortress-like town. In riding across the plain, we had come through much desolation and two ruined and burned villages, and on entering the town, we rode through the *entirely ruined* Christian quarter until we arrived at the American Mission, where four buildings only remained standing out of twelve, the rest being heaps of ruins.

The kindest welcome awaited us here as at every mission station previously visited, and we were soon at home with this heroic little band, every one of whom has faced immediate and terrible death without fear or flinching. This is no figure of speech, for their destruction was evidently intended by the authorities here, if not by those at Constantinople, and it was not by any Government protection (as with Miss Shattuck at Ourfa), but by direct Providential intervention that they were saved.

The soldiers were ranged on the hill-side below, and
the cannon planted pointing at their buildings, which
stood high above the Christian quarter, and the bullets
fell *in showers* upon the premises, while one shell burst
in Dr. Barnum's little study, and we saw the path it made
and where it broke, with its own remains, which he keeps
as a relic.

The officials put the blame for this disgraceful attack
on those above them when not on the Armenians themselves, and justice and truth are things unknown.

And this continued reign of deceit and lies and oppression is never for a moment varied by the opposite. The
poor villagers send constantly to the mission with one
tale of sorrow or another. The Kurds are taking their
harvest, for example; the missionaries tell this to the
Vali, with name of village, date of robbery, &c., who pro-
fesses to be as much interested as they in the good of
the people; and then follows the *invariable* report, which
sounds like an echo of the Sultan's letter to Queen Victoria
last winter, "We have made all inquiries, and we find
none of these complaints are true," and that is the end!

This neighbourhood has suffered more largely in pillage
and destruction of property than any other in Armenia,
and already about £30,000 has been spent here, and over
73,000 people kept alive, and still the needs are almost
as great as ever. There is not a village rebuilt yet of the
more than 150 which have been pulled down and burned.[1]

The tale our missionary friends here (Dr. and Mrs. and

---

[1] A waggon-load of kerosene cans was supplied by the Government to
the Kurds for the purpose, &c.

Miss Barnum, Mr. Ellis, and two single ladies) told us of the time of the tragedy here, was most thrilling. They were all together, with over 100 of their people, afterwards 400 gathered round them, and driven by the fire and the whistling of bullets from one place to another. They had also with them two aged and paralysed missionaries, who had to be carried—a Mr. Wheeler and Mrs. Allen—and they all found a temporary shelter on the top of the roof of the girls' school-room, since burned, which having a little parapet around, was some protection from the observation of the soldiers on the opposite hill. Here they expected and prepared to die together, but after a while, finding the entrance to the boys' school-room, which was on higher ground, accessible, they planned a united retreat thither. In doing so they were deliberately fired at by a Turk, who had found his way to the roof on which they were, as well as became again the targets for a brief space of the soldiers' bullets. The Turk *aimed too high*, else one or more *must have been killed*, his bullet was found in the gateway they passed through afterwards; and as for the rest, the Lord had evidently given His angels charge concerning His servants to protect them in all their ways, and these bullets also did not touch them.

I asked our friends what their feelings were under these terrible circumstances, and I will give you some of their replies as nearly verbatim as possible. One said: "I had always feared death till then, but at that moment all fear was taken from me and death seemed nothing." Another said: "I believe my husband was almost disappointed we did not go, it would have been so lovely to have been taken out of all the confusion and trouble here, by a brief pang, and all together." She also told me she had unloosed her dress in front that a sword should meet with no hindrance in its thrust, and so she should go the quicker. A third said: "My thought was a query whether a bullet going through me, would have force to wound Mr. Wheeler or not" (the helpless friend whom he was assisting to carry); and Dr. Barnum said: "I assure Mrs. H. there was not a woman screamed on our whole ground, and our ladies were as calm and collected as they are now."

The evident Divine protection over these servants of the Lord extended to the scholars also. When the buildings were fired, sixty of the young girls made their escape to neighbouring houses, each of her own choice taking from her small stock of possessions neither jewellery nor clothes, but just her little Bible under her arm. All of these girls returned safely two days after, when the immediate danger was over, and then indeed there was excitement and many tears, and Mrs. Barnum said she was so hugged by the women and girls in their joy, it was hard for her to keep on her feet!

When one contrasts this safety with the dreadful occurrences outside the mission circle, it is the more remarkable. Only a very short distance from Harpoot, for example, thirty-two women, headed by a noble and very intelligent woman well known to the missionaries, had thrown themselves into the Euphrates and were drowned, to escape apparently otherwise unavoidable dishonour, and more than one father played the part of Virginius of old and killed his daughter outright.

The missionaries lost everything they had in the looting

that followed the massacre and fire, but have since bought back a good deal, so that they are living quite comfortably now; but the Government holds out no hope of any indemnity for rebuilding at present, and objects even to small walls being put up, for immediate convenience.[1]

As the post is now going out I must conclude, and remain for us both, yours always affectionately,

HELEN B. H.

[1] A tiny statistical return will assist the imagination to grasp the extent of the desolation in the districts of Harpoot and Palu:—

Statistics for Palu and its Forty-three Villages.

Armenian houses	2,074	Kidnapped girls	43
Number of Armenians	14,878	,, women	152
Houses plundered	2,059	Girls married to Turks	29
,, burned	755	Women ,, ,,	21
,, destroyed afterwards	259	Girls returned	16
Killed	900	Women ,,	92
Wounded	513	Churches destroyed	44
Families converted	474	Monasteries ,,	2
Individuals ,,	3,181	Schools ,,	37
,, circumcised	603	Ecclesiastics killed	16

This list does not include those who died from fear and exposure. The kidnapping represents but a small part of the violence done to women.

Statistics gathered at Gregorian Episcopate for Harpoot and its Seventy-three Villages.

Needy persons	26,990	Forced conversion of men and women	7,664
Houses plundered	6,029	Wounded	1,315
,, burned	1,861	Miscarriages	829
Churches badly injured and defiled	29	Killed in fields and highways	280
Churches burned	15	Persons burned	56
Protestant chapels destroyed	5	Died of hunger and cold	1,014
,, ,, badly damaged	18	Suicides	23
		Martyrs { Bishops	1
Monasteries burned	2	Martyrs { Priests	11
,, damaged	4	Protestant ministers	3
Forced marriages to Turks	166	Teachers	7
Rape	2,300	Men, women, and children	1,903
Forced conversion of priests	12	Total deaths	4,127

Loss of property . . 1,651,956 lires Turkish.

This does not include Malatia, Arabkir, Egin, Charsanjak, Gighi, Palu, Choonkoosh, and Diarbekir districts.

These statistics have been carefully prepared.

LETTER No. XXIV.

HOW TO HELP THE DESOLATED VILLAGES?—CONDITION AROUND HARPOOT—DESPAIR OF THE VILLAGERS—PETITION FROM HOO-I-LOO FOR REBUILDING OF PROTESTANT CHURCH—VISIT TO THE VILLAGE IN RUINS—MEAL IN AN ORCHARD—ASSESSING THE TAXES OF THE DEAD UPON THE SURVIVORS—PLANS FOR FUTURE WORK—VAN, MALATIA, ETC.

HARPOOT, *July* 25, 1896.

DEAR FRIENDS,—One of the most difficult problems in connection with the relief of Armenian distress is that of the villages, and it is difficult in two ways. The first is that these villages are so numerous that to deal with them is much the same as trying to deal with single shops, houses, or persons in a city where there has been murder and pillage. One does not know where to begin, and even if one had a millionaire on the Relief Committee, one would hardly know where to stop. But the second reason which makes it hard to help is that a village *is* a village. It has no walls, nor gates; little or no active government (though that is not always a hardship, when, as in this country, the dogs persistently fraternise with the wolves): and consequently when an attack has once been made upon the Christians either by their neighbours or by outside tribes, the chances are that it will be repeated as often as there is anything worth plundering in the village. In the city, people can combine their strength (even when disarmed by the Government as the first step in a massacre); they can hide a good deal of their property or carry it from place to place; but what can a poor villager do, who owns a very obvious yoke of oxen, and an almost as obvious store of grain? I know of several towns that have been able successfully to resist massacre, but I cannot at present recall a successful defence of a village.

And it is the sense of their helplessness in these villages that makes their and our hopelessness, whenever we give way to despair with them. Here at Harpoot, one looks to the south, from the cliffs where we are perched, across a great upland plain bounded on the south by the Taurus mountains, which we crossed on coming from Diarbekir. This plain is well watered by mountain streams and dotted all over with villages, mostly Christian villages, and almost all of them have been burned and destroyed. For days before the massacre and plunder at Harpoot, the missionaries watched the flames rising from one village after another, as the Kurds and Turks drew nearer and nearer to this doomed city. And what is true of this plain is true of every plain and hillside in this part of the country. It is the same to the north of Harpoot, across the Euphrates, where they have not only carried off the spoil of the people, in oxen, grain, implements, and other properties, but have come back again to plunder them of the oxen purchased for them by some of the relief workers (happily the Government has secured restitution of this last bit of plunder), and are even now threatening them with a renewal of the attacks of last autumn. Is it any wonder that the people feared to till their fields, or that they fear to gather in their harvest, or that they huddle together like sheep, in villages that have not been burned, or where the desolation is less complete? It is a problem to aid them, a more difficult one to secure them from further danger: both parts of the question appear at first sight equally hopeless.

Some days ago we had an interesting visit from some villagers at the south side of the plain, coming from what was once the richest Christian village in the neighbourhood. The men came to the mission (two of them, if I remember, were the deputation) to ask for advice and help. They had been visited, I believe, some time since by one of the Red Cross agents, who had urged them to begin to rebuild their ruined houses, and had offered to start them by giving £5 a piece to the first ten or twenty houses—an excellent plan, and one that went right to the heart of the difficulty. The people, however, had refused the help, not because they were averse to help, but because they were in despair. What was the use of building what would be pulled down again, or of storing what would be plundered again? So the offer was declined, strange as it may seem. It will help you to understand the discouragement of the people.

Their recent visit was on a slightly different errand. There is (or was) in the village a fine Protestant church, which was built four years ago, and is now wholly destroyed, only the bare walls standing. Since the troubles, they have been holding their service in the Gregorian Armenian church, at the close of the Armenian service;

but without much sympathy from their hosts, who have now told them that they cannot any longer entertain them. So the deputation came to Harpoot to know if something could not be done to put their church in order; they did not want their houses built, but they wanted, so they said, a place to pray in, and they begged for help in rebuilding their house of worship. Dr. Barnum told them that there were no funds available for any such purpose, and sent them away, only promising that we would think over their case. I need hardly say that I was very interested in the people who put God first in this way; and while I do not believe in exterior sanctities, I felt the sanctity of spirits that had become prayerful by misfortune, and wished to know more about them. And so it came about that we planned an expedition to them, and yesterday five of us rode across the plain to examine into things for ourselves.

Hoo-i-loo is the name of the place, as nearly as I can write it from sound (for you will not find it marked on any map), and it lies between three and four hours from here (all distances, as you know, are measured by hours with us, like the German Stunde, and an hour stands for the distance covered by a laden horse in an hour of time, say between three and four miles English). Our party consisted of Mr. Gates, Miss Bush, Miss Emma Barnum, our two selves, our servant, and a *zaptich*. There was a cool breeze blowing, and we had a delightful ride across the plain, passing on the way a little Armenian church into which were built two Latin inscriptions, dedicated by Nero to some officers of the third legion. It seemed appropriate to find the name of Nero here! It ought to be inscribed over the whole country-side, and on a thousand broken walls and ruined homes.

When we came to the village, we found that it consisted of about three hundred houses, and that not more than six were standing. All the rest was brown, bare, broken wall of mud-brick, without a roof, and with hardly a door or a window-shutter left. The people began to come around us and welcome us; one of the first women that drew near had lost her hand; there was no more than a stump left by the sword of the destroyer.

We went to the ruins of the church; the roof, as I said, was gone, and every piece of timber in the walls was burnt out by fire. The débris had raised the floor by perhaps a foot. The people crowded round with eyes full of tears, the women telling of slain sons and other pitiful things; the pastor, too, came to talk to us—a fine young fellow, in whom we were much interested. We made the tour of the village, found a little Catholic church similarly destroyed; then I took a lesson in archæology, for I noticed the streets deep in dust from the disintegrating brick, and saw how these mounds or tells were formed that we have seen so many times on our journey. Moreover, it was clear that desolations of this kind had occurred from the earliest times in this country, for how else could we explain the frequency with which such tells or mounds are found? If the people at Hoo-i-loo do not rebuild, there will be a tell formed there within a couple of years.

One single thing I found which had escaped destruction. High on the wall of a ruined house, in the second storey, a photograph was nailed. We sent for a pole and got it down. It was a group of Armenian workmen from a factory at Worcester, Mass., and had doubtless been sent home by some happy emigrant to his relations.

When we had finished our tour of the village, we were taken to an orchard, where they had prepared us a meal. "The robbers have not stolen our gardens," said the poor people. "No," I replied, "nor did they steal the sunshine," at which they brightened up. They set before us great dishes of apricots, apples, plums, and mulberries and cherries prettily arranged with hollyhock blossoms, and brought us milk, both fresh and curdled; and did everything in the way of hospitality that an Eastern people can do so much better than we. And we talked over all their plans, and encouraged them to believe for better days.

I must not forget to state that our study of the village showed that the houses were fired one by one; those that were spared belonged to Turks. They were fired by petroleum, the supply of which was brought in a waggon from Harpoot, by an official of the Government. The man who did it is well known; and I suppose he will be rewarded by-and-by with promotion, if one may judge from parallel cases.

And now what are we going to do for these poor people? We are encouraging them again to rebuild their houses, and shall try to help the foremost of them; and as to the church, who knows but what we may find some way presently to fulfil the desire of their hearts and give them and their pastor a "place to pray in?"

I must not close this letter without saying how delighted

we were to hear that Friends had sent us £1000 for our work here. Some of it may go to the village of Hoo-i-loo. We shall try to be very wise, very wary, and very economical in the distribution of it, so that all of it may go to the neediest people, and none of it may be turned into taxes. By the way, in regard to taxes, we have bad news from Ourfa; the Government is assessing the taxes of the dead upon the survivors! If this is true, it is one of the most heartless schemes that could be devised, and will throw the people back again just as they are rising. And I am almost certain, from the character and position of my informant, that it *is* true.—Your sincere friend,

J. R. H.

Extracts from Private Letters.

If all goes well, I hope to see thee and the rest of our friends in about six weeks' time. Meanwhile letters will still find me if addressed to the Bible House at Constantinople.

J. R. H.

Partly on account of Mr. Atkin's earnest request to us to continue our reports from this country, and partly because I am glad to remain in the country a while longer, I am letting R. return alone. But I shall continue to write you as before, because there is always so much to tell, and now that R. is going there is (perhaps) less need of reticence in using any information I may give, because the Turks despise women so much I don't think they will trouble themselves very much about my doings or sayings. Both our servants will go with R., and I shall accompany him with two of the missionaries to Malatia and then return here with them, leaving the future to Divine guidance. I am so thankful that your £1000 came, or the news of it, before R. left, so that we could consult about its use.

Please do not forget your lonely friend and sister in the service of Christ, now that my so greatly better other self is going home, and let me have a line from time to time, to old address.

HELEN B. H.

LETTER No. XXV.

VIGOROUS PROTESTS AGAINST WESTERN SCEPTICISM—DIFFICULTIES OF RELIEF WORK—REBUILDING OF VILLAGES, ETC.

HARPOOT, *July* 25, 1896.

MY DEAR FRIEND E. W. B.,—We are delighted to hear from Constantinople as well as from thyself the news of the arrival of £1000 from the Friends. I have already sent word as to what we have been doing financially, and will now say a little more on the subject in order that our friends may know exactly what our policy has been, so far as that policy has been susceptible of definition. But first let me say something with regard to the statement in thy last letter, that there are Friends who still talked of atrocities being "manufactured," and others who feared that what was contributed would go into Turkish hands. The first of these difficulties moves my indignation. Do they want me to bring home a collection of people with slashed heads and faces and minus hands and ears? Or to dig up the burnt bones from the caves and trenches into which they have been thrown by the sackful? It can be done, I suppose, but I fail to see how it would add to the evidence of credible witnesses, including ourselves. The fact is that not one half of the horrors of last winter has been told in Europe. No doubt there has been occasional inaccuracy in the newspaper reports, but it would be a mistake to suppose that these reports erred always by excess, and not by deficiency. As to the fear of our funds falling into Turkish hands, that is a reasonable fear. It has happened with other workers in a number of cases, and will happen again, unless our simplicity succeeds in outwitting the rapacity of Turkish officials and magnates. The real answer to this difficulty seems to be in having a right policy for relief. Our policy, then, is as follows: In the first place, we generally avoid giving personal relief; the distress is of such magnitude that any attempt to deal with individual cases can only be compared with the conventional draining of the sea by means of a shell. What we aim at is the reorganisation of social order, which in most cases appears to be hopelessly shattered. It is not the giving of relief in food and clothing, except as a temporary expedient, for if we do nothing more than that, the people are presently back again at the bottom of the pit of distress. If, however, we can encourage them to return to their ordinary occupations, and find them the means of recommencing the task of bread-winning, then we do something that is permanently good. And we do the same when we relieve the social organisation of the burden of those who are quite incapable of self-maintenance, as in the case of widows and orphans. No money can possibly go into the hands of rapacious officials when you buy back a man's tools, or when you provide orphans with food, and shelter them in your own hired house.

In the villages we find the problem very acute; the

houses are all ruined, and the people are afraid to rebuild. Consequently the first thing to be done is to restore confidence by finding a few of the more courageous, who are willing to make the attempt if they are helped with the necessary timber and materials. It is impossible to rebuild a village which would cost £1000 to £2000 in the necessary timber and mud-brick without paying anything for labour, but it is possible to help a few people who are not wholly in despair, and when they begin to build the others follow them like a flock of sheep, and one soon has enough shelters in order for the coming winter. This is what we are trying to do here, and, while I admit that the building of a single village seems almost as absurd as the relief of a single needy person, it is not really so, for the good that is done is contagious, and is sure to be imitated.

I am sending a little account of a visit which we paid yesterday to one of the ruined villages, which will help to explain this part of our programme.[1] It is very difficult indeed to set people to work again in their crafts and trades. Agriculture recovers because nature goes on with her benevolence irrespective of atrocities, and without inquiring who rules the land, but trade and commerce are at a standstill; there is no home consumption, and no export of manufactured goods. The ablest artisans are idle, and it will be long before they find occupation again, and as if to crown their miseries, we hear now from Ourfa that the authorities are beginning to assess the taxes of the dead on the living. I see no way out of this phase of the misery, which results from the rottenness and rapa-

[1] See p. 149.

city of the Government. The case is hopeless; the tree must come down, and the people had better stand from under. Unless they are enabled to make a partial emigration, they will probably be all destroyed. But emigration, like relief, is useless if sporadic; it can only be done successfully on a large scale, and this means Government co-operation.

I hope that nothing I have said will discourage our friends. Thus far we have not been without success, and in Ourfa the success has been phenomenal. The schools which we reopened have now over 1000 scholars, and the orphanage which we started has 70 children, without counting those which have been sent to Constantinople. We should try to do something with the broken machine here, and perhaps at Van. At Diarbekir the people were in such fear that we were not able to plan much permanent work, still I hope that there and elsewhere the suffering has been alleviated. Our friends will see that it was wisely decided to make no new organisation for relief, no organisation can come near to the fitness of the American Missions. If the country can be saved, the foci of its salvation are the mission stations, and in a lesser degree the consulates. No one knows the needs of the people like the Americans, and no one is so busy and so wise in giving aid as they are. They at all events have come to the kingdom for such a time as this. I have just briefly given some of the leading impressions made on my mind by this summer's work. It is a great delight to know that our friends are taking hold of it with us. They may be sure we will do our best to see that their benevolence is not wasted or misapplied, and they will share with us the benedictions, which attend the service, both the outward blessings of those who are ready to perish, and the more precious commendations of the Man of Sorrows that are spoken inwardly.

J. R. H.

P.S.—I am turning homeward in a few days, while H. remains for a month or two longer in the hope of continuing and of extending the work. Perhaps she may go as far as to Van if the way should open.

LETTER No. XXVI.

DETENTION AT HARPOOT OWING TO DIFFICULTIES OF TRANSIT—STORY OF A YOUNG ARMENIAN, JUST RECOVERED FROM HIS WOUNDS, NOW PUT IN PRISON—QUESTION OF THE RELEASE OF THE MANY IMPRISONED ARMENIANS; IS BRIBERY LAWFUL?—A HARD CASE—EXAMPLE OF THE EARLY CHURCH—THE MISSIONARIES' DECISION—LETTER FROM OURFA—TEACHING THE WOMEN AND GIRLS—WORK FOR THE ORPHANS—"HARRIS HOME" IN FULL OPERATION—ONLY THOSE ENTIRELY ORPHANED CAN BE HELPED.

HARPOOT, *July* 30, 1896.

DEAR FRIENDS,—We are detained here by a concurrence of such events as make travelling in Turkey difficult; for example, the Government is harassing us over the travelling papers of our servants, and I have already spent a Turkish pound in telegraphing; then one of our baggage waggons has been seized by the military pasha, with the promise that he would find us another, and it turns out that the other is broken down and needs repair; and, last of all, one of the waggoners who has turned up is badly drunk, and as these fellows killed a woman this morning, as she stood at her own door, by their reckless driving, we don't feel like employing a drunken man belonging to a craft where the sober ones are so risky. So we are stopped till to-morrow morning, and perhaps by that time some of the difficulties will be cleared away.

Almost every day brings some fresh story of injustice.

One of the most pitiful of recent cases was that of a young Armenian who came to call here; he belongs to a wealthy family, but in the recent troubles he lost father and brother, and almost all their estate : he was wounded in forty places, and you will not be surprised that he has taken eight months to recover; rather you will be surprised at his recovering at all, and will pronounce it an irregular proceeding. And now, just as he is recovering, face to face with a ruined business and a desolated home, the Government have arrested him on a charge of conspiracy, and are searching his house. The ground of this proceeding is, that he wrote a letter to a friend in Erzeroum asking him to assist a poor fellow either to find employment or to *escape to Russia*. This letter has been intercepted, and is considered evidence of conspiracy. The pathetic side of it lies in the fact that the man has already suffered to the utmost limit, but this does not satisfy the persecutors, and I suppose they will not spare him unless he can bribe his accusers and his judges.

Talking of bribery and its prevalence in the social order, we have been dealing with it in the mission lately as a burning question, which had to be faced, not merely theoretically, but practically. (We are all of us sound theoretically, it is no question of abstract ethics.) The question arose as follows. As you know, the prisons in Turkey are filled with leading people from the Armenian community, especially with Protestant teachers and preachers, who are the chief agents of civilisation in this country, and therefore the favourite victims of the Government in their attempts to reduce the Armenian people to primitive serfdom and savagery. In Malatia, and in Arabkir, two neighbouring towns, there are many Armenians in prison, all of them known to be innocent of the political offences with which they are charged, and none of them as yet honoured with a trial, although they have spent two-thirds of a year waiting for it.

Well, last week the leading Armenians out of prison succeeded in opening communications with the authorities for the release of the leading Armenians in the prison. An intimation was made that the major part of them would be released on a payment of £80 Turkish. The people were prepared to close with the offer. They raised £40, and came to the missionaries (and I suppose to ourselves) to aid in the good work of emancipation of the brethren. The terms were not bad; the Government would allow all the prisoners except four or five to go out, reserving only the handful in question for trial, in order that the world might see that it was the Armenians who made all the trouble, from which it looks as if they meant to hang five, but were not particular which five.

Here comes the rub! The missionaries say (with one or two exceptions), "We have never bribed, and we never will. If we once begin this, even with good ends in view, there will be no end to the claims that will be brought forward, and we shall encourage injustice, &c.;" others pleaded the importance of the liberation of the preachers and teachers at this crisis; and, for the sake of argument, I reasoned on their side, pointing out that we do not pay people to do wrong, but to do right; just as in the Customhouse, when you have nothing contraband, you pay to be let alone, and are guiltless of any wrong to the revenue. Also I quoted the Apology of Aristides, who says of the early Christians that if any of their number are imprisoned for the sake of their Messiah, they help him to the best of their ability, and if it be possible that he be liberated, they liberate him. These words imply, at the time when they were written, the maintenance of the prisoner from outside, and his release by what we should call bribery, but which in the East is named backsheesh.

However, I do not think our friends here thought the argument convincing; they have indeed supplied the needs of the imprisoned by money, food, &c., but shrink from direct interference with the distribution of justice and with the repression of injustice.

Probably they are right, especially as their choice of a selected number of prisoners would involve the execution of the remainder—a grave responsibility—and in the end we all agreed, I think, to do nothing; we naturally come to that conclusion in the special case, because we do not feel that we have any funds to spend that way. It is, however, very interesting to find oneself discussing a problem which must have often presented itself in the early Christian Church, and which, I imagine, they usually settled in a different way to ours. The Armenians do not understand our attitude, but then they are so accustomed to pay blackmail for everything, that they have hardly reached the point at which the problem asserts itself.

One thing, however, is clear to me; that just as one is obliged to suffer with the people when we are not free to struggle for them; so if we cannot open prison doors with golden keys, we must find some other keys, in the shape of lawful persuasion. If only we might be able to do something in this work!—With every good wish, your sincere friend, J. R. H.

Extracts from Letter from Miss Shattuck.

OURFA, *June* 27, 1896.

PROFESSOR AND MRS. H.

MY DEAR FRIENDS,—We can't get permission even for Burbulian to come here as preacher. The poor people are all wanting a pastor. Mr. Knadjian and the old preacher of the Protestant Syrians preach for us on the Sabbath; the church reopened during the week. The women teachers I have had to increase, and also to put in teachers from house to house, so many of the women are intent on learning to read. The large girls, many of whose betrothed have been killed, are in our school, and have one appointed to teach them at as fast a rate as they can follow, and meanwhile to read the Gospels to them giving the life of our Lord, and they are required to give back from memory what they can.

I had not called at the Palace since the week you left till last Friday. The wife of the Pasha inquired particularly for you, Mrs. H., and sent salaams. The son informed me that "an American traveller is expected here, name not in mind." I suspect it is some one who has come and gone, as long after Messrs. Wistar and Wood had left us our inspectors reported their "intended visit to Ourfa."

The sums you have given I indicate by enclosed receipt. Including Yevnige's Vohan, we have in Harris Home twenty-nine, *i.e.*, twenty-seven children. We have the necessity of opening a second home for girls, and I am doing this now (Monday). We took in no girls last week for want of room. We have several on the list, also boys to be received immediately. I am having stone-men enlarging kitchen in our back yard, so we yet are far from order and quiet, but since it is the season for sleeping outdoors we get on tolerably well. We have eighteen, and four to come in to-day; all are complete orphans but one, and the sons of the matron at Harris Home. We dare not yet open the way for half-orphans, though many widows unable to care for their many children want to give us one. The *unbounded confidence* in any plans I make for these poor women and children throws upon me a very heavy responsibility. The Lord grant us all wisdom and grace for what is our part to carry on the great work. —Very affectionately,

C. SHATTUCK.

LETTER No. XXVII.

ARRIVAL AT MALATIA—EXTENSIVE DISTRESS THERE—A PARADISE CITY—ACCOUNT OF THE MASSACRE—THE RUINS TO-DAY—HOW TO HELP THE PEOPLE—THE REFORM COMMISSIONER—LARGE MEETING IN A GARDEN—DEPARTURE OF J. R. H.—PASSPORTS FOR THE TWO SERVANTS—INTERVIEW WITH SHAKIR PASHA, AND WITH THE PASHA'S WIFE IN THE HAREM—A FRIENDLY BEY WHO HELPED THE ARMENIANS — EMBROIDERY WORK — BOARDING OUT THE ORPHANS: FIVE POUNDS FOR ONE YEAR—THE PRESS OF TEARFUL WOMEN—CONFISCATING THE FRUIT IN THE GARDENS — PERSECUTION OF KURDS WHO REFUSED TO MASSACRE—MISS BUSH AND DR. GATES.

MALATIA, *August* 3, 1896.

MY DEAR FRIENDS,—As I am now on my way home, I suppose this will be the last circular letter that I shall be able to write. We arrived here safely on Saturday night, after a two days' journey over a mountainous country, from Harpoot. "We" stands for Miss Bush and Mr. Gates of the American Mission at Harpoot, Professor Tenekedjian of the Euphrates College, and our two selves. All of them are here for purposes of relief, and I only wish I could stay with them, for the trouble in Malatia is very great, worse than in any place we have visited except Ourfa, and in some respects it is worse than Ourfa, although the sum total of misery and wickedness is less. However, if I cannot stay another three or four months as I could wish, it is a satisfaction to know that the work is in such good hands in this district, and that good care is taken to make the help given such as will be of permanent benefit. Up to the present time 7732 people have been assisted in this city; but the work has now passed out of the stage of immediate relief to sick and wounded or starving individuals, and our friends have to face the problem of putting together as best they may the broken pieces of the social fabric. You will understand what is involved in this if I tell you the state of the city a little more in detail.

Malatia is the most beautiful city I have yet visited in Asiatic Turkey. If we use the word Paradise in the old Persian sense of park or garden, this place is or was a paradise. It is a succession of beautiful gardens, planted with poplar trees and every variety of fruit trees, and watered by streams that descend out of the neighbouring mountains. Almost all the houses stand in the midst of their own gardens, and the impression of the city as one approaches it from outside is more like that of a long stretch of woods than of an inhabited place, as the houses are almost entirely hidden away.

Before the troubles began in this place the relations between Moslems and Christians were very friendly, and there was no revolutionist propaganda of any kind, as there is also no trace of any such movement in the majority of the inland cities of Asiatic Turkey. But the fire of fanaticism is easy to light; a part of its fuel was found in the increasing prosperity of the Armenians, and the match was set to the fuel by a direct telegram from the Sultan. As the Moslems are five to one, it is not surprising that the massacre was a successful one; what is surprising is that the Christians were able to defend themselves for many days by firing from the roof of the chief Gregorian church upon the attacking Turks, when they had only old-fashioned guns with flint-locks, whereas their persecutors were armed by the Government with Martini-Henry rifles.

I could tell you many tales of horror in connection with these days of violence and persecution. The estimate of Christians killed varies from 2000 to 4000; most of the leading Protestants were slaughtered, and the flesh of their chief men carried round the market for sale at 20 paras (about 1d.) the oke ($2\frac{1}{2}$ lbs.)! (I may say that I thought this last piece of atrocity must be apocryphal, but we have heard it from four different quarters.) In one of the churches fifty people were burned, and no doubt the great Gregorian church would have been the scene of a massacre like that at Ourfa, if it had not been for the heroic defence made by the people who were imprisoned in it.

The Protestant church and schools which I have visited to-day is a mere pile of bare walls. Of the houses in the Christian quarter 560 were destroyed, and up to the present time I cannot find one case of rebuilding, such is the fear in which the poor people live. Add to all this wreck of property in the destruction of houses, churches, and schools, the wholesale robbery of everything that could be carried away, the violence done to the women (600 girls and brides carried off to Kurdish and Turkish houses), and the ruin of families by the murder of the men, and you will get a faint idea of the state of things in Malatia. As I have said, it is in some ways worse than Ourfa. At Ourfa the houses are built of hard stone, upon which fire had little effect; but here the material is sun-dried bricks made of mud, with roofs of poplar beams, and such houses it is comparatively easy to destroy.

What is to be done with it all? It would take an immense sum to rebuild the ruined quarter; I cannot see how any relief committee can take the responsibility of it. Yet, on the other hand, some shelters must be found for the people against next winter, or they will die like sheep. They cannot live in the gardens when the frost and snow come, nor sleep on the ground without beds, as many are doing now. The only thing I can think of is to stir the people out of their lethargy by offering some help towards building to selected individuals, and so stimulating the rest by their example to build themselves some rude shelters. Then there are the widows and orphans and the ruined schools, &c. &c.

Our friends will have their hands full during the next few weeks, as they proceed to the closer analysis of all this distress; but they have good experience of the work from their toil during the past eight months, and we shall be able to help them in many ways in rolling the load from off the back of this crushed and suffering community.

We have come here at a good time, as Shakir Pasha, the Reform Commissioner, is at present here investigating into the abuses of Government and the misfortunes of the people. We hope to have an interview with him this afternoon, and, if possible, shall urge the release of certain prisoners who are still under ward though they are known to be perfectly innocent. Perhaps we may also obtain from him permission for the rebuilding of the ruined church and schools. We shall see. And here for the present I must stay my pen.—Your sincere friend,

J. R. H.

P.S.—We had a good meeting with the Protestants yesterday. As the church is in ruins, the people met under the trees in a garden. They were very attentive. When we proposed that they should sing a hymn they shook their heads; since the troubles they had not been able to sing. However, some of our party started a hymn which they all knew very well, and presently they joined in. The number of orphans in the town is very great; they say at least two thousand.

J. R. H.

Further Account by H. B. H.

MALATIA, *August 6th.*

R. left us on the 4th, our entire party and the British Consul, Mr. Fontana, accompanying him for two hours, when we were obliged to return. Our two servants accompanied him, having obtained *teskerehs* for the rest of the journey by the good help of the Consul; and these permits will prove a valuable aid to his safe return to Constantinople, so that we have now no more fear of prison for them, or detention on their behalf for him—a danger which for the last month has been threatened for both of them, as Griva the cook lost his road-paper when floundering in a mud-hole we went through near the Tigris, and the Pasha at Harpoot refused to grant another.

R. and the other gentlemen had an interview with Shakir Pasha before he left, but they did not get as far as to be able to intercede for the prisoners, but Miss Bush and I fared somewhat better in a visit to Mrs. Shakir and the harem yesterday. We were able to put the matter plainly before her, and Miss Bush assured her that she had known the imprisoned pastor for years, and highly esteemed him and most of the others in prison. Then I put in my word in testimony of the good work done everywhere by the American missionaries, both for Christians and Moslems, and I said *they loved all.* "Not the Turks, I fear," she said, with a slightly sarcastic smile; but Miss Bush said most emphatically, "Yes, the Turks also, and we earnestly desire that all may dwell together as brothers." How much of what we said sunk in we cannot tell, but we felt God's presence and help as we sat talking there in the shady harem tent, and sipping first tea and then sherbet, and we believe good must and will come of the visit. This lady, we should say, is a Polish Roman Catholic, and the Pasha's chief, though not his only wife. How she reconciles her position with any sort of Christian profession I do not know; we looked upon her simply as a *Turkish* lady. Her position must in any case be most painful and anomalous.

After visiting her, we went to the harem of the governor of the city, and got on satisfactorily, and again after that visited the ladies of a very friendly Turkish Bey, the only one in the city who has really befriended the Christians, but he has done so all through at the risk of his life, and at the time of the massacre had his house full of Armenians; and we saw a woman whose hand had been nearly severed by a sword, the wound having been at the time dressed by the Turkish ladies of this home. An Armenian woman and a sufferer was in the room with us during our reception, and lovingly treated by them; and you may imagine *how cordial* our intercourse was under the circumstances, and how we all united in the desire that such events as have just transpired here might never again be repeated while the world lasts!

Now that R. has gone, I am only remaining, as you can easily imagine, to help the people a little longer, working with the missionaries, and also doing some things alone. For example I am ordering a good deal of sample *embroidery* to be made (as at Ourfa and elsewhere), hoping to get a sale for it in England and America. It is quite unique here, and used for divan covers; but I am having squares and round pieces done for cushions, footstools, and strips for borders of curtains.

Then I *must* do something with the money of the Friends' Fund for the hundreds of widows and orphans—of course taking advice with the missionaries and Consul—whom the other friends are unable to attend to for lack of funds. Instead of starting an orphanage as at Ourfa, I want to give two or three fatherless and motherless children to such widows as have lost their own or have room to take them, and already there are a hundred waiting! Five pounds each would keep a child for a year and be a little help to the widow, and this means £500 at one stroke! Of orphans whose fathers only have been killed there are thousands, and of these many *must* also be supported; £500 would be none too much for them, and then it is only for a year; and what then? Happily there are very good people here to superintend this work, both men and women who once lived in every comfort, had beautiful houses, and are educated according to the standard of the country, and who also are full of deep sympathy for their people, while themselves are suffering with them, and who can be *fully trusted*.

Oh! if you could only see and hear these people! The women's eyes are *always full of tears*, and for the most part the men's too, only farther back; the women cling to one's dress, they catch and clasp our hands, they *will not let us go* without a promise of help, and yet they evidently hate to trouble us, and are not a bit like common beggars; but what can they do? We seem to them like messengers from above, and they flock around so that often there is not room to move for the press; and what can we do, in our turn, but still hand on their sad, sad beseeching cry for help to those at home who love Christ's poor?

Another piece of injustice I must tell you before I close. R. has written of the beautiful fruit-gardens, and the fruit is most abundant; but since he left we have heard that the Turks have stationed people to guard the Christians' gardens (outside the city where the largest are) to prevent the owners picking the fruit, on the threat of having their throats cut. So they cannot eat their own fruit.

One more tale and I have finished for this time. Yesterday, outside Shakir Pasha's encampment, were a number of Koordish women begging. To my surprise Miss Bush gave them each a small alms; and as this is not her practice, even with the Christians, I naturally inquired the reason; and then she told me these women belonged to a Koordish village near the city which, for some reason, had refused to help with the massacre (the only one out of a hundred who did refuse). Because of this humanity, regular troops were sent who destroyed and burned and pillaged their village as if it had been a Christian one! They therefore have a special claim upon our sympathies, and you will no longer wonder at Miss Bush's action.

Miss Bush, I must tell you, is a second Miss Shattuck, who has lived twenty years in this country, and has visited most of the chief towns, and all the people love her; she and I are likely to work together pretty closely now that I am alone, which is a great privilege and blessing for me. Dr. Gates, President of Euphrates College, is also with us, a very interesting man and devoted missionary.

We shall probably stay here ten days longer, making arrangements to send more money after we leave; and we shall probably also return by Arabkir, where there is also great need, to Harpoot.—Yours affectionately,

H. B. H.

LETTER No. XXVIII.

OUR LAST DAY IN MALATIA: A BUSY CROWD — SELECTING FIFTY ORPHANS OUT OF FIFTEEN HUNDRED—DEPARTURE—GOODNESS OF SOME MOSLEMS—THE ZAPTIEHS—JOURNEY BACK TO HARPOOT BEGUILED BY HYMNS — WELCOME AT HARPOOT—PLANS FOR VAN.

HARPOOT, *August* 19, 1896.

DEAR FRIENDS,—In our last joint circular from Malatia you heard of R.'s departure. I can now report his safe journey as far as Marsovan, and no doubt very soon, almost as soon as this reaches you, he will be on English ground once again, and able to talk with you face to face! It seems strange to continue my lonely circulars after losing him, the chief actor in our past travels, but as I am writing on the condition of this afflicted land and beloved people quite as much as to describe personal experience, I will do my best to keep you in touch with matters here so long as I remain, and as I move from point to point to carry you with me in my travels.

Our last day in Malatia was our busiest, I think. All our premises were in a constant crowd, in which it was difficult to say who were coming and who going! Turkish commissioners and *zaptichs*, Gregorian priests, Protestant deacons! The architect, yesterday out of prison, busy suggesting how to rebuild the ruined Protestant schools, so that on Sundays they can be also used as church, to hold 1000 people. The young preacher, also just released (the joint effect of the visits of the British Consul, Mr. Fontana, and Shakir Pasha, to Malatia), going in and out among the crowd with a constant smile on his fine open countenance. The still imprisoned pastor's wife trying to rejoice in the freedom of her husband's late companions, but with a twitching of the mouth, and repressed tears in the eyes, because her dear one is still, with one other, held in thrall for no other conceivable or pretended purpose, except to save the appearance of opening the prison door too widely (and also, if possible, to secure a bribe).

Here are the Building Committee, deep with Mr. Gates in plans and projects for rebuilding the houses of the town, a grant of money for this purpose having just been telegraphed from Constantinople. There is Miss Bush in an inner room, writing down from the lips of an eager-looking young woman seated at her feet an account of heroic courage and self-sacrifice during massacre days, a tale which will equal anything on record almost of womanly heroism, and which I hope to send you by-and-by. And in the midst of all, here come trooping up the stairs, and on to the verandah, accompanied by a number of women caretakers, the band of orphan children from whom, with the help of the committee, I am to select the fifty orphans I have promised on behalf of the Friends' Relief Committee to care for during one year. Each little creature salaams in a way that tells of a high civilisation somewhere in past history, if not of present culture, and stands waiting my verdict,

and then for each pleading voices are lifted up,—and
these Armenian women know how to plead! Fifty out
of fifteen hundred good orphans are not hard to select,
except that so many must be rejected, and I will have
none but those whose fathers were actually killed in the
massacre. It is hard to say "no" to many, but this is
more than counterbalanced by the joy of accepting some;
and I only wish the dear friends, who have contributed to
the Fund from which they will be supported, could have
seen the delight and heard the grateful words of the
crowd, as one after another of the silent little candidates
for succour were selected, and their names written down.
We did not finish our work until the stars were overhead,
and had to begin again by daylight next day; many
visitors attended us during our early breakfast, so that
instead of our usual quiet devotional time afterwards, we
had prayer in Armenian for the company, offered by the
native preacher.

Then we mounted our horses, which were all in excellent spirits, and rode out of the beautiful, though ruined,
town in the quiet morning, the streets lined with
Armenians to bid us farewell, and the market-place with
Turks, who saw us depart no doubt with great satisfaction. Once again, however, I must bear witness here to the
goodness of some of the Moslems in the time of trouble,
in Malatia as elsewhere. One man who came to see us
had sheltered several hundred Christians, and another had
kept sixteen in his house. I believe with all my heart
that there is good stuff hidden away in the ordinary Turk
behind a mass of evil. For he is a slave to those in

authority, and to the cruel part of his creed, and these two forces hold him in bondage to that which is bad; under better auspices I believe *much good* would appear, and the same remark applies to the Kurds, only that they are more savage still.

Our *zaptiehs* are almost always helpful, and I think glad to be with us. One who came part way from Malatia to Harpoot poured out to Dr. Gates a tale of woe—*zaptieh* woe, of which who ever thinks?—which was sad to hear; no pay for a year, and hurried here and there, tired and sick at heart; no home life, no comfort of any kind: they almost quarrelled for the chance of who should come with us to get our food and fee, at one stopping place.

Our journey back to Harpoot was unmarked by any incident worth recording. The heat was intense, such as we never feel in England, and we rode from eight in the morning till five in the evening under the blaze of the sun, with hardly an hour, in the middle of the first day, to rest and eat by the side of the Euphrates before crossing, under the flickering shadow of a lonely tree; and in the second day in a little khan, where for lunch we drank bowls of hot sheep's-milk, and ate a very little native bread, and the luxury of that lunch I shall, I think, never forget!

The road was good and broad most of the way, it being the central road through Turkey, and we rode four abreast, and Mr. Gates and Miss Bush sang, besides many sweet hymns, "Way down upon the Swanee River" and other old-time songs, which brought back to my remembrance my own girlish days. What I enjoyed most, however, was the hymn—

"From Greenland's icy mountains,"

and the stanza commencing—

"Waft, waft ye winds His story,"

made my heart thrill with joyful anticipation for this land as for all others, so that I could not but look backward and ask our *zaptieh* if he did not think the missionaries' song very good.

But I must not be discursive. In the afternoon of the second day we met the entire Harpoot Mission Station, six in number, come out three hours from the city to meet and welcome us back. Thus Oriental lavishness in welcoming courtesy is engrafted upon the graciousness of Western manners, and makes unitedly a most charming compound.

Shakir Pasha is here now, and I am endeavouring to negotiate through the Consul a journey under the shelter of his wing to Van, taking dear Miss Bush with me, if the Board permit, but this is quite uncertain, and we may go to Arabkir instead, whence the cry is loud for help.— Yours affectionately,

HELEN B. H.

[H. B. H. adds in a letter: Please do not slacken interest in the country and people because of my husband's return, for their very existence depends on our keeping up our work for them, and *not growing weary*. He will be able to do more for them in England now I feel sure than were he still here, and I know you will still continue to pray for me in my solitary lot.]

MEMORANDUM.

Notes of Information from J. R. H. to a Special Meeting of the Society of Friends held in London, Sept. 4, 1896.

I. — GENERAL FEATURES OF THE H.'S MISSION — THE AMERICAN MISSIONARIES' GRAND WORK — RECONSTRUCTION OF THE BROKEN SOCIAL MACHINE — HOUSE-BUILDING — THE WIDOWS, ORPHANS, AND SCHOOL CHILDREN—SAFE ADMINISTRATION OF THE FUNDS — THE OURFA WORK — SPIRITUAL LIFE AMONGST THE PEOPLE: MANY POWERFUL MEETINGS—THE PROGRESSIVES OF THE EAST — FELLOWSHIP IN THE CROSS — THE CONSTANTINOPLE MASSACRE: PERSONAL EXPERIENCE.

II. — NARRATIVE OF JOURNEY FROM HARPOOT — MALATIA: A RUINED COMMUNITY: FIFTEEN HUNDRED ORPHANS AND FIVE HUNDRED WIDOWS—GREAT MEETING IN AN ORCHARD; HYMN-SINGING: BREAKING THE SPELL OF DESPAIR — HELP TO THE SCHOOLS: THE SECTS UNITING — HELP FOR THE ORPHANS — RESTORING OF HOMES — ARABKIR AND GURUN: A TRIANGLE OF DESTRUCTION — H. B. H.'S CONVICTIONS FOR VAN — SIVAS: A TERRIBLE MASSACRE—TOKAT, AMASIA, AND MARSIVAN.

I.—GENERAL NOTICE OF THE MISSION OF J. R. AND H. B. H. TO ARMENIA.

J. R. H. described some of the delays and difficulties they had met with, but which had proved generally helpful in the end, *e.g.*, they could not have well got into the country earlier than they did, or at a better moment. They had indeed been wonderfully guided.

Their great care in going to work silently had not

perhaps been understood at first, but events had shown it was wise.

They had been able to visit every city they designed to visit; once only having met with prohibition as to route. They soon found that no fresh organisation was wanted: the Armenian question is an American one. The civilisation of Asia Minor is American; it is covered by a network of American agencies; there are good colleges and schools, medical colleges, and schools for training preachers. The same thing is going on as in Bulgaria: the Americans are training the future rulers of the country. The Armenians were getting wealthy, enterprising, full of skill and commercial activity, thus provoking the hostility of the Turk, and furnishing a seed-bed of persecution. Our friends always co-operated, where they could, with the American missionaries as well as with the English Consuls, and never had he met with more beautiful co-operation than with the Americans, who were always at their service.

It felt like putting together a clock that had been smashed: it was a piece of broken society, and you had to study the conditions of life, beginning at the bottom—food, clothing, shelter—working up. Suppose in one of our towns, one half of the shops were looted, one fifth of the population dead or wounded, one fifth of the women widows, it would be very difficult to put it all together again. Whole trades had disappeared: you want to shoe a horse, all the smiths are dead; tools are stolen, and the workmen have nothing, and cannot get them back. The social problem was therefore very difficult, requiring much adaptation and skill. What could they do? Put together those who belonged together—try to construct a commonwealth out of ruins!

The capital necessary for this would be, indeed, almost boundless; it was absolutely impossible to undo the work that the Turks and Kurds had done by giving money. You come into a village where every house but five or six are in ruins, and in the midst of these ruins the people are living and sleeping, with very little to cover them. The villagers say, "It is useless: the houses will only be pulled down again if we build them;" but you converse with them, and you see that if some would build a few houses others would follow suit. This is the true evolutionary line. Our friends supplied not money, but materials for building, the people found labour; they built five or six small houses, and this furnished a nucleus: others would then build. It would take £10,000 or £15,000 to rebuild a village; they could only put down £100 worth of raw materials as a beginning.

They devoted attention to this because the winter was coming, and they saw that many would die of cold as well as starvation.

Then as to the widows and orphans: No one else was working for them, that part of the community was incapable of recovering itself: men could begin again and go to work; the child is helpless, and widows nearly so. In Malatia there were 1560 orphans and 500 widows, and almost every Christian house was ruined. Imagine the state of fear and despair in which the people were. Our friends took hold of the question, and began to organise, collecting some of the orphans into little groups, and setting women to take care of them. The children were running wild about the streets, *playing at massacre*, and learning everything that was bad. Our friends induced the Gregorians and Protestants at Malatia to combine in a school committee, and they then furnished accommodation for 1500 children for the present.[1] They saw no other way of restoring the social machine.

Something permanent was thus done. Others had given away corn; the harvest was being collected, and was a rich one. They had not therefore given much for food, and never gave money, lest the Turks should take it away. The Turks had indeed made strenuous efforts to get at the relief funds, and not always without success, but so far as he knew they had got none of theirs.

They had gone over the length and breadth of the country, having ridden 1500 miles: H. B. H. would probably ride another 1000. Some journeys were very rough and dangerous; they could not have done it without a sense of Divine help, and the prayers of the people of God, which they felt were given them. We should not now diminish our intercessions, but remember the one left behind, who had taken the hardest part of the work, and was bearing the burden. May the Lord preserve her and bring her back!

Some of the work had developed in a remarkable degree, especially at Ourfa. They came there at its worst point.

---

[1] Obstacles have been thrown in our way in the prosecution of this plan, which we hope will be surmounted.

The condition was something like that in England after the Black Death. The price of labour had risen, and this made revival easier. The Turks tried to get complete control of trades, &c., but could not. Our friends undertook 20 orphans to begin with, and tried to restore the school for 700 children; now Miss Shattuck writes there are 70 orphans and 1100 children under care, and the city has largely recovered, and trade and industry are reviving. The place where things were worst has now a better prospect than most.

He had had many precious and beautiful opportunities of speaking to the people, through an interpreter—many large and powerful meetings. The Turks sent watchers to try and find objectionable matter, but exhausted their subtlety in seeking for such. He had two or three thousand people at a meeting, and they would listen all day, if you would speak: like the early Friends' meetings, where there was no clock but the celestial ones.

The Gregorian Armenians were as a rule willing to help them; sometimes they were suspicious and would not, but generally otherwise. H. B. H. had a large women's meeting at Malatia: the priests were present and sympathetic.

After these meetings they seemed to get hold of the length and breadth of the community: every one comes and tells you their trouble, and in a little while you can take stock of the situation, and begin to put the works together.

There is a good work to be done amongst these people: they are not savages, but the progressives of the East.

They know your sciences, your mechanics, and are rapidly imbibing the principles of Protestantism. There are many deep and sincere Christians, loyal to Jesus Christ; many have borne every discredit and dishonour for the Great Name. In one case, a man at Malatia was riddled with bullets in the form of a cross, that, as they said, Jesus Christ might find him if He wanted him. A woman came to J. R. H. to ask why God permitted such dishonour to His Name: she was referred to the Gospel, where Jesus was reviled and taunted on the cross. The people were thus down at the lowest point in regard to faith, and in danger of gravitating to despair. He hoped that their service had helped the people, and had shown them that God rules through all.

There is still need of caution at present in any publication, as a hostage is in the enemy's country.

J. R. H. arrived at Constantinople on Sunday, August 24th, and for two days was engaged in trying to see ambassadors and other persons of influence, but without much avail. Miss Kimball, from Van, with whom and her two companions he had travelled from Samsoun, while walking down the streets of Galata, said, "These streets will run with blood before long." They did so. It was known that something was going to happen.

J. R. H.'s personal experience in the streets during the massacre on Wednesday generally confirmed the newspaper accounts. It was systematically organised: the carts were ready, and the wards of the city were taken one after another; the porter of one hotel said ninety-six carts of dead bodies passed the door before 4 A.M.

on Friday morning; not a single male Armenian was left, it is said, in one quarter: they were hunted like rabbits.

II.—NOTES OF J. R. H.'S JOURNEY.
Chiefly a Summary of Circular Letter No. XXVII.

Taking up the thread of our narrative from Harpoot, July 30th: We went from Harpoot to *Malatia:* Shakir Pasha, the Reform Commissioner, was there; the British Consul went also, and some missionaries from Harpoot. There was much excitement in the place on our coming, the whole town came out to view us, and we were welcomed remarkably.

We were much surprised at what we found. At Harpoot it had been a country difficulty, a village question, many of the houses were not destroyed; the lives had been mainly spared,—a few hundred people killed. In Malatia it was a contrast. A city, in which the destruction of life was awful, almost all the houses were down; it was like Ourfa again, where there were very few Christian villages outside the city.

We visited Shakir Pasha, and called on the Mutessarif, —it was he who gave the direct orders for the massacres; he killed the Christians even in the Government buildings, ordered them out in the street and had them shot under his eyes, when they begged to be spared. We asked permission of Shakir Pasha for H. B. H. to pay a visit to his wife. She is a European (Polish). . . .

After these arrangements on the Saturday, we looked about the city, a beautiful one, a city of gardens—every house in its own garden, with streams of water running through; perhaps 40,000 inhabitants. The houses were not as at Ourfa of stone, but of mud bricks and poplar beams, some very beautiful, but destroyed easily, simply burnt out; 500 or 600 had gone, only two or three Christian houses were left,—we had one. The people were living in gardens and on the ground. The place had been visited by the Red Cross Mission.

There are no missionaries living at Malatia: it is under the Harpoot station, the preaching all done by natives, and well done. There are 1560 orphans in the city, and over 500 widows. In one ward of the city there was only one male Christian left. Christians are perhaps one in nine of the population; there were killed altogether about 3000 (November 1895). Very little news of this came to Europe. The people defended themselves in the Armenian church, barricaded themselves on the roof of the church with the stones found there, and kept up fire for eight days, till the Government was obliged to send them protection.

The missionaries and ourselves examined into the state of the city. On the Sunday we went to see the Protestant *church*, which we found ruined and the school destroyed; it was a large and a beautiful church, not yet completed. The pastor was in prison; we tried to get him released. We had a meeting in an orchard, where there was a verandah; the people came, and the missionaries also, a large crowd in the open air under the trees. I spoke, of course through an Armenian interpreter. I asked the people to sing a hymn; some hymns are not allowed by the Turks (as, "Jesus shall reign where'er the sun"). They said, "We can't sing; we have not sung anything since the massacre." I said, "You must sing:" a lady started a hymn, and by-and-by the whole congregation joined in. This broke the spell,—the apathetic despairing mood of the people; they had "hung their harps on the willows," and we got them down. I spoke, it was a very good meeting; they said it was what was wanted, and their condition had been spoken to.

Then the people began to visit us, and we learned the state of the city. It was like Ourfa, but with the complication that the people were houseless, and there was not the same number of wounded.

We left after three days. H. B. H. stayed on and investigated the whole of the city for orphans and widows. We examined the question of the *schools*. I promised to put a roof on the Protestant school-house, so that they would meet there on Sundays for worship. Understanding that we were going to help the Protestant school, the Gregorians also asked help. We made them a similar offer to that which we had made at Ourfa. "Were the Gregorians prepared to join the Protestants in a common School Committee?" Yes, they were now willing. So we put our heads together and reorganised the school, to take 1500 children, Protestant and Gregorian. The people were penniless: Armenian schools are generally independent and self-supporting; now the children were running wild in the town. We arranged this, getting a builder to roof the school-room.

As to the *Orphans:* We could not found an orphanage

(had no firman from the Government), so we did as before, got some of the best women to take the children into their homes, and to look after them at an estimate of so much per head; twenty to begin with, and I telegraphed afterwards to take more.

Houses had to be built. Of course we could not rebuild a city, even though labour is cheap. So we set a good example to stimulate them to rebuild, provided materials for certain houses—maybe we shall build ten or twelve houses to encourage the others. The people in winter will be making mud bricks for themselves. "Will they be destroyed again?" Well, we must relieve; we can't speculate as to the future. The people said, "It is no good, the houses will be pulled down, and we shall be plundered." Miss Bush of Harpoot was put at the head of the schools.

All our money is kept in the mission safes, and none of it, as far as we know, has been lost.

Malatia forms a triangle with other two towns (*Arabkir* and *Gurun*) that have been very roughly treated. Arabkir was visited by the Red Cross Mission early in the spring, when typhus was raging (2000 cases), and they had done chiefly medical work.

H. went back to Harpoot, travelling with two missionaries (Mr. Gates and Miss Bush) to that place. She is staying on with a prospect of further relief work in the country.

I worked my way down from Malatia to *Sivas* by Saturday night, five long days' journey. There was a very terrible massacre there, the Protestant pastor was shot and many leading Christians. I put up at the American Mission. On Sunday I preached in the Protestant church, and there were other services also throughout the day. I stayed to meet the English and American Consuls; they were all of one mind, the situation is intolerable, a disgrace to England.

I reached *Tokat* two days after (where Henry Martyn died); there had been no trouble there, but the people were threatened.

Amasia came next, after two days more. The people here were plundered, but helped one another. No outside aid required.

I was at *Marsovan* for Sunday, and preached in the church. The town was badly treated. Much relief money had been received, and all put into industries. Fifty looms were started, and thus they got all the money back again (the relief work has therefore become self-supporting). I found a difficulty as to drugs; one of the lady missionaries was providing them out of her own salary.

I came on to *Constantinople* on August 24.

LETTER No. XXIX.

PRIVATE LETTER OF THANKS FOR UNEXPECTED CONTRIBUTION—BUILDING OF SCHOOLS, ETC., AT MALATIA — THE PEOPLE SET CHURCH BEFORE HOUSES — ONE THOUSAND CHILDREN TO BE ACCOMMODATED — A JOINT SCHOOL BOARD — UNION OF THE CHURCHES.

HARPOOT, *Sept.* 1, 1896.

BELOVED FRIENDS,—"Before they call I will answer," &c. The lovely letter of encouragement and the cheque for £250 seemed like a direct reply to my telegram from Malatia, though posted probably before that was thought of. How good God is thus to fulfil His promises of old, and how lovely of you to have the needs of my now lonely work so much in mind! I do thank you most warmly and shall use it all, or nearly so, for the purpose indicated in my telegram, and already I hear with the inward ear the multiform sounds which accompany building at Malatia.

If permission is granted by the local government for rebuilding the schools, which on Sundays will be used for church, the shape of them will be something like this—

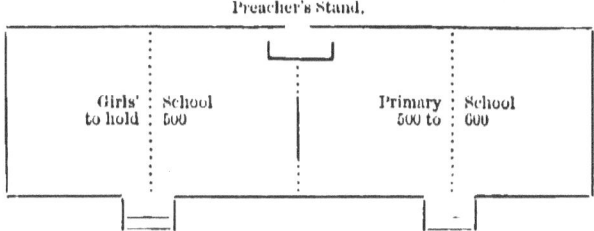

The dotted lines show wooden partitions which will be removed on Sundays, and the preacher can then have an audience of 1000 or more very well. They get in about twice as many people to the square yard here as in England, because there are no chairs or benches; all sit on carpets as close together, if need be, as is physically possible, and you never saw such a sight as they present when crowded, especially the women.

We have sent the first instalment of money, and oh how glad they are! for this is a religious people, and it is true that they begged that their church might be rebuilt *before their houses*—and so it will be—though I rejoice to say the Duke of Westminster's Committee has allotted £2000 for rebuilding houses, and that work will also begin soon. I have also advanced 50 liras for the roof of the boys' school in the market-place—a new building at the time of the massacre, only needing the roof. Now they will soon get this up, and 500 boys will then be taken from the streets (indeed they are being gathered together now), and so there will be accommodation for 1000 children.

The people will themselves provide the teachers, and Miss Bush and I appointed the school board—part Protestant, part Gregorian, with a Protestant as chairman, and Miss Bush as real, though absent, head, just as Miss Shattuck at Ourfa. This union of the ancient and more modern Churches in joint work is a most blessed thing. The Gregorian priest spoke of it with enthusiasm after the women's meeting Miss Bush and I had in their big church (1500 at least) as what he longed for—the uplifting, the teaching, the enlightenment of his people. It was at his entreaty that the boys' school was undertaken and the committee formed, and now they are working away with a will.

Do not think, beloved friends, that this is any less relief work than feeding the bodies of these poor sufferers. Without public worship or schooling, they do not feel as if they are really living, only existing.

I was extremely touched at the account of that young Christian servant and her noble gift. I read it to our assembled company of missionaries, and I do not think there was a dry eye. I have made her gift a special donation for aiding the most destitute of the Christian women here, under two of the lady missionaries, so that every penny will be prayerfully expended.—Your sister as always, H. B. H.

Armenian Relief Fund.

[I add a report of relief work done in the Harpoot district, which will enable friends in the West to understand the condition of the Armenians in that district at the close of the present summer.— J. R. H.

HARPOOT, *September* 3, 1896.

DEAR FRIENDS,—For nine months a constant stream of benevolence has been flowing into this country for the relief of the sufferers from the sad events of last November. It is now a fitting time to look forwards and backwards, to recount the good that has been accomplished, and to forecast the needs of continued relief.

The field of which Harpoot is the centre contains a much larger proportion of desolated towns and villages than any other. In 256 towns and villages we have given relief to 74,805 souls. The money distributed amounts to L.T. 27,544. The greater part of this has been paid out in small sums for the purchase of food; each family received a sum varying according to the number of souls—ten piastres for every adult, and one-half that amount for children.

In this way relief has been distributed three times, and in some places four times, during the winter: and it is the universal testimony of the people that they owe their lives to the relief money sent to them from England, America, and Europe. They are constantly invoking God's richest blessing for those who, for love of God and humanity, have cared for them in their distress.

The money thus given has been largely paid from our hands into the hands of the recipients. Favoured by an exceptionally mild winter, the people have come a journey of two and three days to receive the help which has kept them alive. Our premises were thronged daily by crowds of applicants waiting their turn. It would have been impossible for us, with the small number of workers we could command, to have fed this army of 70,000 souls in any other way. We could not go to them, nor send grain to them; but they could come to us, and they could buy food for themselves with the small sums given to them.

At the same time a bureau of industrial relief for women was opened under the care of Misses Bush and Seymour, where the destitute women of the city, and refugees who had fled hither for safety, received small wages for cutting cloth and making garments to be given to the destitute; 3630 pieces of bedding were given out from this depository, and 18,228 suits of cotton underclothing. Where 70,000 souls are in need, it is very obvious that this supply is wholly inadequate. In some cases money was given to the people to enable them to buy back the beds which had been stolen from them, but thousands of families slept on the ground without covering all through the winter, and in many other families the sick and the well occupied the same beds.

Employment was given to men also in clearing away the ruins of our burned buildings, repairing the Protestant graveyard, making roads, and the like, at wages which would barely provide bread for their families.

L.T. 120 have been expended in giving relief to refugees not reached from any of our relief centres. Many of these were in a deplorable condition. The storm broke upon them when they were away from home. Stripped of clothing, without money or food, ignorant of the condition of their families, they came to us for aid to make their way back to their desolated homes.

From this same fund we have aided the refugees who were crowded together in the cities to go back to their villages and find employment there, and we have cared for those who came here to obtain relief. To these last we gave sums equal to one or two cents per night, with which to obtain food and shelter. They slept in the khans, huddled together like sheep to keep warm, for they had no covering to protect them from the cold of winter.

L.T.10 was expended in redeeming girls and women from the hands of the Kurds who had carried them off captive. Others were redeemed in the same way by the help of special gifts or by their friends and relatives.

L.T.116 have been expended for the relief of Gregorian priests and teachers. The condition of this class is often most deplorable. The communities are no longer able to support them. They are unused to labour, and have no trade with which to support themselves. Their condition is one that appeals strongly to our sympathies, and I should be glad if some special provision could be made for them.

Through the winter we employed a physician to care for the sick; we sheltered many sick and wounded in a temporary hospital, and furnished food and medicines. The whole expense was small, L.T.33.

With the opening of spring we felt that relief methods must be changed, and that efforts must be made to start the people in business, so that they might become independent of aid from abroad. Our missionary force was too small to grapple with this problem, but at this juncture the agents of the Red Cross arrived upon the field, and organised three expeditions to Arabkir, Charsandjak, and Palu. These expeditions were most helpful in just the lines of greatest need, inspiring the people with hope, and furnishing them with means of resuming their former occupations. The very thought that some one cared for them gave hope to the people and proved a stimulus to them. Since the departure of the Red Cross agents the same work has been carried on in Chemeshgesek and Malatia. Time is needed for the country to recover from such terrible ruin as has been wrought. For a long time the people seemed completely paralysed. They were left not only helpless but hopeless.

Now, as it is the season of harvest and fruit-gathering, we are suspending relief work for a season, with the exception of efforts to put the people in the way of earning their own living, and we are trying to estimate how far it will be possible for them to care for themselves during the coming winter.

Much has been accomplished in the lines we have indicated, and the number of those who must still receive relief has been greatly diminished. In Malatia the list has been reduced from 7700 to about 2000 souls, and in other places a great many will be able to get through the winter without aid. But there are some features of the situation which make it inevitable that there should be much distress during the coming winter, and which make it necessary to continue relief measures even though it be on a reduced scale.

In the first place, many have no houses to shelter them. When cold weather sets in they will be no longer able to live in gardens as they have been doing through the summer, but will be forced to huddle together in small and unsuitable quarters, where disease will break out and carry off many. This is notably the condition of Arabkir city, where 1561 houses were burned, and only 621 remain to the Christians. If some provision is not made for sheltering the people, last year's epidemic of typhus fever is almost certain to be repeated there. More than 600 died of this disease last year; the fatality is likely to be worse this year, because the people are more enfeebled. Many villages are in the same condition as regards shelter. This is the most pressing need at the present moment.

The second need is that of help to start in business. Many are still unable to provide themselves with tools or capital so that they may resume their former occupations. In Arabkir weaving was the principal industry. The Red Cross gave some 150 looms. Others had repaired old looms or provided themselves with new ones. With the opening of the winter there will be a demand for all the cloth they can make, but they have not the capital to purchase thread for their looms, and the merchants who formerly furnished the capital have been impoverished, so the looms stand idle. If L.T.2000 could be invested in thread, and distributed among the weavers of that city, it would set that industry going, and furnish employment for many of the widows and orphans there.

In Choonkoosh business is at a standstill. The people were artisans and tradesmen who pursued their business in the villages, travelling all over the region through the summer and fall, and returning to their houses in the winter. Since the massacres they have not dared to go out to the villages, and they lack the capital to make a start in business. Malatia was in the same condition, but a recent visit there did much to restore confidence, and to set things going. A visit to Choonkoosh was also planned, but the Vali objected to our going by the direct route on account of danger, so the visit has been deferred. It would be hard to find a better investment for relief money than is offered in this line of furnishing men with a small amount, seldom exceeding ten dollars, with which to begin business. It is better to put a man in the way of earning his own living than to support him by alms.

The third feature of the situation is one that calls for serious thought and effort. It is the large number of widows and orphans left without any bread-winners on whom to depend for support. A careful canvass of the city of Malatia and seven near villages shows that there are 1883 orphans and 630 widows there. The number in Arabkir is said to be even larger. In the village of Harboosi there are between thirty and forty orphans who wander about the village as the dogs do, eating, sleeping where they can. Every town and village furnishes its contingent of widows and orphans, and the villagers are too much engrossed in the struggle to provide bread for their own families to care for these helpless ones as they would ordinarily do. What is to become of them?

In Malatia, Mrs. Harris, the wife of Professor J. Rendel Harris of Cambridge, England, has gathered samples of embroidery wrought by the women, hoping to find a market for it in England and America. Anything that can be done to furnish lucrative employment to widows and orphans will greatly relieve this saddest feature of the present situation.

Some efforts have been made to care for the orphans. Ten have been sent to the Deaconess' Home in Smyrna, and a few more will shortly be sent to Broussa and Constantinople. Through Mrs. Harris' kindness some fifty have been placed in homes in Malatia for one year. But the multitude uncared for is hardly affected by these efforts.

I think the most feasible plan of caring for them is to find homes for them in Christian families, who will receive them and bring them up until they are able to earn their own living. This would involve an expense of about twenty-five dollars (£5) per year for each child. It should be stipulated that the children should attend a Christian school, and wherever the number of orphans in a place will warrant it, some faithful man or woman should be appointed as guardian to visit the children in their homes, and see to it that they are properly brought up.

In some cases, perhaps, ten children could be placed in the care of a worthy widow. Some children could be received into our boarding-schools if provision could be made for the expense. Our schools are already so heavily burdened that we could not assume more without help. The cost per year would be about forty dollars (£8) for a boy or girl. This plan has the advantage, that a beginning can be made at once. Whenever the money is provided a boy or girl can be at once cared for either in a family or in our schools.

After all that has been done, or may be done, in these lines, it is certain that there will be at least 20,000 souls in this field who will need help to get through the coming winter. The provision hitherto made for beds and clothing is wholly inadequate, and there will be great suffering as winter comes on unless help can be given for this.

Then, too, many can make no adequate provision of food for the winter. In the Charsandjak region the harvests are scanty, and it is estimated that by the time the people have paid their taxes little will be left for them. In all quarters the Government is now pressing hard for taxes which have been suffered to remain in arrears until the time of harvests. Now the officials, who have received no salaries for months, collect the taxes with the greatest rigour, and do not scruple at any treatment of the people to extract money from them. A great part of the harvests will go to satisfy the claims of the Government. Moreover, there are many who have no fields, to whom the harvests bring no relief. This is the case with a large proportion of those who dwell in the cities of Malatia, Arabkir, Palu, and Harpoot. Even now the cry for help for food from Arabkir is bitter, and growing increasingly urgent. It is difficult to forecast the future, but I think it will require at least L.T.12,000 to provide food for the starving during the winter, and if the need of beds, clothing, and shelter is to be met, very much more will be required.

(Signed)   C. F. GATES.]

LETTER No. XXX.

JOURNEY TO VAN PUT ASIDE FOR THE PRESENT—HEMMED IN AT HARPOOT—SIGNS OF TROUBLE AROUND—PRESENCE OF H. B. H. "A SAFEGUARD TO THE TOWN"—COLLEGE FLOURISHING— H. B. H. ILL WITH MALARIAL FEVER—THE GREAT NEED OF HELP FOR THE ORPHANS.

Appended.

I. APPEAL FROM MALATIA FOR MORE HELP FOR ORPHANS.
II. THANKS FOR HELP IN REBUILDING CHURCH AND SCHOOLS AT ARABKIR.
III. LETTER ASKING PERMISSION FOR PROTESTANTS TO WORSHIP IN GREGORIAN CHURCH AT MALATIA.

HARPOOT, *September* 16, 1896.

DEAR FRIENDS,— After my confident expectation of being able to make the proposed journey to Van in the company of Shakir Pasha's party, you may be surprised to find me still dating from Harpoot. Our change of plan was certainly a great disappointment and surprise to me, but I will simply narrate events.

We had planned to follow two or three days after the Marshal, so as to avoid travelling on Sunday, and because he expected to remain four or five days at Palu, where we were to join the company (leaving Harpoot on Monday, August 31). Mr. Fontana, the Consul, brought up our *teskerehs* on Saturday evening; the Kurdish muleteers (six of them) were on the grounds with their animals, our tents were ready, and baggage and provisions all packed, when a telegram from the British Embassy, telling of the events of the 27th at Constantinople, changed the aspect of affairs. The Consul would have still let us go, travelling under the circumstances not being more dangerous than staying here in his judgment, but the mission party felt that in the uncertainty of events here, *they must all keep close together, and not leave the college premises.* This opinion was quite united and decisive, and as I could not travel alone without dragoman or interpreter, it decided the question for me too.

So here I am until the way opens for some new plan. Humanly speaking we are hemmed in on every hand, and I will tell you briefly that the people all around are greatly disturbed, and we hear of trouble in various quarters, near and far. I myself do not believe that it will be anything like last autumn and winter, for I believe the Turkish Government is on the alert to prevent; but no doubt terrible threatenings are being uttered on one side, and believed on the other, and so people are bringing their goods to the college for safety, and the Consul has asked for a largely increased guard of soldiers for us.

In his letter to the Vali making this request, he gave, as an added reason for the precautions, the fact of an English lady being for the time here, and the great importance of her safety. This troubled me not a little, for, as you all know, I have no confidence for myself in the protection of guns, &c., and so I wrote and asked the Consul to tell the Governor *I* had *no* fear for myself and did not wish any more soldiers sent here on my account. The

Consul replied very courteously that he would remember my wish, and added that he himself considered my presence here a great safeguard to the place. This is a new light on the subject, and perhaps it is for this purpose I have been permitted this detention.

In spite of all the trouble around, however, the college has just reopened with more attenders, both of boys and girls. than ever before, about 300 boys and over 200 girls, and most of these are paying for themselves. This indicates, I think, the hopeful and elastic character of the people, and their great love of education. Does it not? And this is going on in face of a mandate from ———, lately received, to the Government here, to discourage the Protestant propaganda, which has had the effect of shutting up one school and place of worship already, but not the one that we gave £40 to repair before R. left, for that is, I thank God, open, and full of children, and when I am well enough I am going to pay it a visit.

For you must know, dear friends, that, in company with several of the dear missionary party, I have been down with some kind of malarial fever since our journey was given up, and am rather weak still; but do not trouble, as I am all right again.

I am sending with this a letter (No. 1.) from Malatia, or part of one, about the fifty orphans I arranged for there, out of Friends' funds, for one year, the sum being £200. You will see they want £40 more, and no doubt next year will hope for a repetition. As I am still reserving some money for other places, I do not feel that I have the means of acceding to their request, but I send the petition, that if Friends' Committee wish these added ten to be taken on, they may communicate directly with the "modestly-shining" Miss Bush herself, whose address is simply—American Mission, Harpoot, Turkey. I thought the letter so characteristic of the people, that, apart from the request, you would like to see it.

I also send a long document, of which extracts might be sent round in a circular, about the general state of the *orphan* question. The friends here think the way we are doing at Malatia is the best way to grapple with the difficulty, and better than for the mission stations to try and take such masses of children in, or to form orphanages. I send the paper specially to make you all feel the terrible necessity of providing for as many as is possible of these bereft little ones for the next few years, and if at Ourfa and Malatia and Van (?) Friends can maintain fifty or sixty for four or five years at £4 each, it will be a work the beauty and blessing of which no words can ever tell.

The Malatia letter makes no mention of Friends as their benefactors about the orphans, though we impressed upon them again and again from whom the help came; this you must forgive, for poor human nature looks to the *immediate* hand held out, and so, no doubt, we have had more than our share of gratitude, though you are mentioned, I am glad to see, under the general title of "philanthropists."

I send also a note of thanks (No. II.), which really belongs to Mr. and Mrs. Crossley, for help to repair the Protestant church at Arabkir. This is really being done now, and will soon be used, for which we may give great thanks, in view of others forbidden. The one at M., about which I wrote when there, and for which help to rebuild is given and in Dr. Barnum's hands, is again stopped, after leave having once been given. Now that the hot weather has gone there is nowhere for the Protestants there to worship under shelter, which is grievous, and no prospect of any, so I have made bold to send a personal request to the two priests and two leading Gregorians that they will kindly allow the Protestants to worship in their great church once during Sunday, till they can build for themselves. The note (No. III.) of Miss Bush making this request for me I also enclose, because it is itself quite Oriental in style, I think.—With much love to all dear friends, yours always,

H. B. H.

No. I.

MALATIA, August 13, 1896.

MODESTLY-SHINING MISS BUSH.

DEAR SISTER IN CHRIST,—This first time of our writing, we reveal our and the orphans' fathomless gratitude to you and to the gentle and good-hearted lady, Mrs. H., and to all philanthropists.

After your departure, the orphan committee immediately put their hands to the work by going about among the different quarters of the city and observing the orphans and their guardians, according to the arrangements which you had directed. From the money you gave us we give to each of the fifty orphans 33 piastres (about 5s. 4d.). We required of their guardians that they should be kept clean and should have home training and be taught to work. For one or two who had no natural guardians we found places.

As we said, again we repeat—Malatia will remain always grateful to you. Your benefactions are not to be forgotten. You (the missionaries) were the saviours of Malatia from being destroyed by famine, therefore it is indebted to you for existence. You satisfied the hungry; may the Lord reward you, we have no compensation. Now, also, you (meaning Mrs. H. and her friends) care for orphans. We pray that the Lord will reward this also with His abundant gifts. What you have done are such benefits as not only such a fallen city as Malatia cannot recompense, but even a people burdened with good things could not.

You also will witness, and we told you when here, that to examine into the condition of orphans required time, which it was impossible to find then. After you went, when we made examination, there were found many worthy orphans serving your purpose who had been altogether forgotten. Our conscience now tortures us as to why these more worthy of sympathy should have been forgotten. For long it will torture us, modest sisters, if for these remaining miserable ones we do not offer a petition to you. If possible, we entreat, be pleased to give the privilege of adding ten orphans to the fifty now cared for, by which these wretched forgotten ones also will be comforted, and you also, without doubt, have gained the right of being yet more rewarded of God.

Our gratitude and respect offering to you, we remain, the ones praying with you,

No. II.

Translated from Preacher Bedros Hachadooryan's Letter from Arabkir, August 22, 1896.

"For the £30 sent by modestly-shining lady, Mrs. H., for the renewing of our chapel and schools we are very grateful. Be pleased to be the interpreter of the grateful feelings of myself and the people, and to offer her our deep thankfulness. This great favour done to us, and this graceful service for the glory of God, will remain an indelible memory upon our city and in our hearts. We entreat that the Lord reward her."

No. III.

Translation of Letter from Carrie E. Bush to Gregorian Armenians in Malatia.

"Mrs. H. salutes you and says, 'Because I have tried to gladden you and to care for you, in a friendly way I wish to entreat something of you; that is, that you will give permission to the Protestants to worship once on the Sabbath in your Holy Trinity Church until they are able for themselves to build a chapel. Because I will help them to build, but at present they are hindered.

"'If you give this privilege, I know that to God and to us it will be pleasing, and I will especially pray that in return for this brotherly love and sympathy you may be rewarded by the protection and peace of God.'"

LETTER No. XXXI.

SUMMARY BY R. H. F. OF PRIVATE LETTER FROM H. B. H.—SYMPTOMS OF FURTHER MASSACRES—THE BLOW FELL AT EGHIN—HARPOOT THREATENED—STATE OF TERROR—THE PROTESTANTS TO BE SUPPRESSED—REPORT OF THE EGHIN MASSACRE.

PRIVATE letters were received on October 10 from H. B. H., dated from Harpoot, Sept. 21. The account she gives of the present situation is distressing in the extreme. The people had begun to have some hope, the widows were again gathering the little interests of a home around them and their half-clothed little ones; the men were settling into work; the children were collected from the streets and again placed in schools, and the churches were regularly filled by the saddened remains of their former congregations. Gleams of a brighter day seemed breaking upon the unhappy people; but alas! these have been dispelled, and again the dark shadow of massacre has risen. The symptoms which ushered in last year's terrible events are again present, massacre is in the air; there are whispers, communications, reports, letters. A day is spoken of, "no protection, no quarter this time:" must the woes of the flock of wretched unarmed sheep, ready for the slaughter, be yet further prolonged? So in Harpoot came this terror upon them: the women were wailing, the men praying that they might die by the bullets of the Kurds, and not by torture. They knew not where the blow would first fall. It fell at Eghin (Sept. 15); so at Harpoot there is a respite.

But at Eghin the scene was terrible. Most of the Christian houses were burnt, many of the best and most respected townsmen are killed; a father and his three sons, for example, who have all left widows except the youngest. Some of the women and girls, to escape dishonour, flung themselves into the river. Alas! for the unutterable woes of these people. Our friends deem this act to be justified: "It is better to fall into the hands of God."

Some assert that the Armenians always themselves bring on these troubles, that they do something to bring down reprisals. H. B. H. (speaking for the localities she knows) states that this is a falsehood patent to all who witness the events. The massacres are planned beforehand. The Armenians have been deprived long since of their arms, they are defenceless and cowed. Do the sheep attack the wolf? They have no recourse, no place to flee to. Abject submission is their attitude, and their only possible policy.

And now Harpoot is trembling. The fiery trial of November last was not enough. The Turks are saying "Wait a little, wait until the harvest is gathered in. By the middle of October this will be done, and then ———." Imagine with what feelings the peasants are reaping their fields, and the poor wives and daughters are going about their daily tasks!

The face of the country has changed during the past few weeks. H. B. H. says she has herself gone through more suffering in these three weeks than in all her previous life, but she adds, "It is not of ourselves that any one thinks in this mission circle," though danger is great. The British Consul is doing his utmost for their and her protection, yet their safety, even as to life, is far from sure, and she desires that no warlike reprisals should be taken if aught happens to her. "But these poor terrified creatures, who have no Government to protect them, no Consul to interfere for them, only an unseen foe hungering for their extermination,—God protect, and pity, and save them!"

"I think God held me here," she continues, "that I might hear and see what before we had but *heard* of. Also I can comfort the people a little, and sympathise with these dear and noble missionaries. Last Sunday I held a meeting for women after the other service, and I think about 200 were present, and I spoke to them on 'overcoming faith.' Afterwards *how* they gathered round me! weeping and smiling at once, so grateful and loving, and now I am to speak to them again to-morrow.

"An edict has come to the Governor here, and no doubt to all other places where American missionaries work, 'to suppress the Protestant propaganda,' so there is a general stopping, or forbidding to open, of these places of worship and schools. But on the college premises worship still goes on as usual, only it is far more fervent, and in spite of everything there are now over 600 students, boys and girls, on the grounds, whose laughter at play, or singing in the schools, often comes to my ears as a strange contrast to everything else around.

"In less than a fortnight I may attempt the journey to Sivas, where other missionaries are, and where most earnest invitation calls me, and thence as way shall open, Van being, humanly speaking, impossible.

"Possibly I may go to Eghin instead of to Sivas, as the accounts that are coming in of the distress there are terrible. But the road is very rough, and the missionaries say I have not the physical strength."

Our friend goes on to suggest possible means to help in this crisis, and some steps which have now been taken, the nature of which cannot be stated here, but these means are followed by very earnest thoughts and prayers that they may be blessed. She concludes, "I will go anywhere and do anything, and meet any one, for the sake of this suffering people. I am at your and God's disposal."

A telegram has been received stating that H. B. II. started from Harpoot on Oct. 5 for Arabkir and Eghin, hoping to go on to Sivas, and so to the Black Sea coast, homeward.

A short report, by one of the Harpoot missionaries, of the Eghin massacre has been received, and is given below.

R. H. F.

HARPOOT, *Sept.* 23, 1896.

I am very sorry to report that a great calamity has befallen the city of Eghin. There is no town in the interior with more wealth probably and with better houses. There were about 1000 Armenian houses and an equal number of Turkish. Of the Christian houses it is said more than 600 have been burned. The estimate of the killed is from 800 to 1000.

Eghin is one of the few places that was spared during the devastation last autumn. A large ransom was paid to the Kurds at that time, and the Turks and Christians joined in defending the place.

The official version of the late affair is (I have it from superior officers), that the Christians gathered in large numbers in the churches, Sunday morning and Monday morning, and prolonged their services so that the suspicions of the Turks were excited. On Tuesday the Armenians set fire to some of their own houses in the upper part of the city, and began to fire on the Turkish houses, killing a soldier.

The facts seem to be these. The local governor, who is a native of the place, with two or three others has represented to the Governor here that there were some seditious characters there, and it is claimed that some Eghinlees in Constantinople were concerned in the late disturbances there. The Vali spoke to some of the Eghinlees who live here in regard to it, and they wrote to their friends, and they said there was only one suspicious character there, and he was a Harpootlee, and had been sent away. Correspondence between the Eghin, Harpoot, and Constantinople authorities has been going on for several weeks, and it would seem that the Constantinople Government was persuaded that there was a seditious element in Eghin, and orders were sent to eliminate it. A few days ago, the Kurds, but not in large numbers, threatened the place, but they were sent away by the soldiers. This was repeated two or three times. On Monday the 14th instant they again appeared, and the Christians had begun to distrust their own neighbours and closed their shops. Tuesday morning, as the shops were not opened, the Governor sent criers throughout the city, to proclaim that the Kurds had been dispersed and the Government would assure the perfect safety of every citizen, and every person was commanded to open his shop and resume his business. Upon this, the shops were opened and business resumed its usual course. About noon a single shot was fired, and the slaughter immediately begun. The gun is supposed to have been the signal, although the Turks claim that it was fired by an Armenian. Massacre seems to have been the first thing in order; plunder, and the burning of houses, later. It is reported that many women and girls threw themselves into the Euphrates, which flows just at the foot of the city.

The *Kaimakam* has telegraphed that two or three thousand

persons are helpless and hungry, and he appeals for aid. The Government will probably do a little for present relief, but it will be only temporary and inadequate. Eghin seems to have suffered even worse than Arabkir and Malatia.

Some prominent Turks intimate that the probabilities are that trouble is in store for this region, and they say that if it comes, it will be worse than last year.

LETTER No. XXXII.

I.

INTENDED VISIT TO EGHIN — FURTHER REPORT OF THE MASSACRE THERE—TWO LETTERS FROM PROTESTANT ARMENIANS IN NEIGHBOURING TOWNS.

HARPOOT, *Sept.* 29.

As we are hoping to start for Eghin to-morrow, I have no time to write a circular letter, but enclose this week's "News Notes" (respecting the Eghin massacre), the same that goes to all the stations of the American Missionary Board here (for each station issues such notes weekly or fortnightly).

I also enclose two letters from A. I think the one from the pastor *most* touching.

I did not write last week because we were in the midst of a panic, not knowing what an hour might bring forth; we do not know even yet that the Vali will allow us to leave, for of course it is hateful to the Turks to have us go to see, and seek to alleviate, the misery they have caused, and the Vali is sure to make every possible objection; but the news from Arabkir is so pitiful that we are going to try and get there for next Sunday, three days' hard ride over one of the worst, if not the worst, of mountain roads in Turkey! If we go I shall probably not return here, but go on to Sivas; that is, if I can get escort.

I am getting better from the fever, though rather weak yet; but I shall gain strength on the saddle and in work, I know.

P.S.—9 P.M. I am within the last hour in receipt of a very kind and interesting letter, which speaks of *three* sums of money sent me by your committee, and so far I have not heard of either of them having arrived at Constantinople! (£300, £400, and £500). How grateful I am to Friends for these large sums I cannot tell! I shall probably use a great deal in Eghin, and do it with such a thankful heart; but even now I must not speak too confidently of going to Eghin, for, remembering Van, I tremble yet. If we go I shall not attempt writing from thence, but wait till I reach Sivas, a place of comparative safety.

H. B. H.

10 P.M.—Dr. Gates has just been up to say that £300 has reached Mr. Whittall. Again many thanks. I shall draw it at once.

II.

Further Report on the Eghin Massacre.

HARPOOT, *Sept.* 29, 1896.

The news which I gave last week concerning Eghin was derived chiefly from two candid Turks who were there at the time of the massacre—they left before there was a definite knowledge of the extent of the disaster. I do not know of any persons who have come from Eghin since that time, but letters received by to-day's mail more than confirm the first reports, and agree in fixing the estimate of about 2000 as the number of the killed. More women and children in proportion seem to have suffered this fate than in any previous massacre of which I know. Many of the dead were left in the streets for days as food for dogs, and large numbers were thrown into the Euphrates. They have been seen floating down the river forty or fifty miles below the city. In some cases whole families have been obliterated. Two thousand is a large proportion in an estimated population of between 5000 and 6000 Christians.

The letters give the number of houses as 1100, and of these it is said that only about 150 are left. The carnage of blood and fire lasted from Tuesday the 15th to Thursday the 17th September.

All the testimony concurs in showing that the massacre was official, and that it was wholly without reason. There was no disturbing element, except in the imaginations of a few officials. They had alarmed the central government. The Vali and the military commander were in the telegraph office here most of the time from the beginning to the end, communicating with Eghin and Constantinople. As far as I can learn, the people made no resistance whatever, and no Turks were killed, except possibly later, in the division of the spoils. There were no Kurds in the place. The work was done by citizens and soldiers. The massacre extended to several of the Eghin villages, but we have no details.

The local government is constant in its assurance that no further massacres will take place in this region, and a good deal of energy is shown in restraining the turbulent element. Five people were killed in the Aghun villages, one of them a priest; but the timely arrival of soldiers prevented a general massacre. After all that has happened, it is not surprising that the Christians have no sense of security, and that they are unnerved by fear. The destitution of the coming winter threatens to be almost as great as last year.

We were extremely glad to welcome Mr. Browne from Boston. His coming gives us much cheer and courage. He hopes soon to visit Eghin with some other members of our circle.

The schools have opened prosperously with nearly seven hundred pupils. They are mostly in rented premises.

III.

Translation of Letter from Protestant Preacher at ——.

Sept. 20, 1896.

MODESTLY-SHINING LADY, MISS BUSH,—Your Sept. 12th letter I received, and became aware of its contents. I cannot write as before, because my mind has become completely weakened, and is not able to work.

My spirit, this troubled spirit of mine, I have wholly given and committed to the Lord. As yet the expected peace I have not. Pray that the Lord will cause to cease the perplexity and trouble of my heart, and grant to the whole world, peace. What shall I say of the disturbers of our peace? The Lord grant them grace. The Lord give to our illustrious Sultan more wisdom, that he may skilfully find means to return peace to this land.

Finally, we have the condition expressed in 2 Cor. i. 8. Encouragement and discouragement combined have melted and wasted us. One encourages us and says, "Do not fear, there is nothing." Another, from another direction, brings gloomy news to cast us down. The Lord grant to our uneasy hearts, peace; and to our country, quiet.

I am sorry to say that, through fear, many have become ill and have forgotten hunger. The local government encourages us, but no heart has remained in us. Whatever may be, the Lord lead.—Yours in Christ,

K——.

IV.

Extract from a Letter from an influential Armenian Protestant at ——.

"You write it as the opinion of Dr. Gates and some of the brethren that at present no one will die of hunger. This is a mistake for this town. The widows and orphans here are many of them without work, and therefore wholly uncared for. If you were here you would see with your own eyes a crowd of orphans who wander through the streets to beg. But who gives? Who has anything to give? What is this, and evils like this, which come as the result of hunger? It is not necessary to mention other contemporaneous evils which spring from hunger and poverty. I wonder if these are less painful than death, though that, also, is threatened. —— has need of bread as long as the people have not commenced work.

"Upon all this, the days of fear have commenced again. Our G—— M—— brother, when coming from a village, was wounded with a dagger, and the poor man is now in bed. Things threatened like this are not lacking. The Lord have mercy!"

LETTER No. XXXIII.

I. LETTER FROM J. R. H., NARRATING HIS JOURNEY OUT OF ARMENIA IN AUGUST, VISITING KHANGAL, SIVAS : MARTYRDOM OF PASTOR —TOKAT : TOMB OF HENRY MARTYN—MARSOVAN—AMASIA : CLIMATE OF PONTUS : TERTULLIAN ON MARCION—SAMSOUN.
II. REPORT ON REBUILDING VILLAGES.
III. FURTHER REPORT ON EGHIN MASSACRE.

I.

Clare College, Cambridge,
October 22, 1896.

My dear Friends,—I have been asked by some of you why I did not give some account of the journey from Malatia to the Black Sea; so I take up my pen, rather late in the day, to satisfy your inquiries, and to say just a few words about the places through which I passed and the people I met. You will observe that this part of the way has to be written in the first person singular, and if the word "we" ever comes in it will be the editorial and regal "we," with its affected and deceitful multiplicity.

You will not expect me to say anything about the difficulty of leaving Helen behind me; it is sufficient to say that she rode with me from the modern Malatia for several miles along the North Road, until we came to the ancient Malatia, the Melitene of Church and other history, an interesting walled city, whose ruins I had no time or heart to investigate; and under the walls of the city we parted, as we believed, in the Will of God, with the good hope of meeting again before long, in the same adorable Will.

The road to Sivas lay for five days over a dreary succession of mountains. The scenery was quite equal to the average of what one had become accustomed to in the central parts of Asia Minor, that is to say, the rocks were limestone and the like, scarcely decently clad with vegetation, and very often as bare as the scalp of death, and blazing as if it were high noon on the Day of Judgment, as indeed it ought to be, if that day is ever going to materialise. Those people who praise the paradisaical character of Turkish scenery, and the speakers who perorate about paradises turned into pandemoniums, seem to me to cast the mantle of their laudations somewhat too liberally over the nakedness of the country. It is not a rich country; too often the interior is like the bare hills of Judea, a country decidedly not flowing with milk and honey.

I passed through very few villages on the way to Sivas. One of the most interesting to me was a town which I turned aside to see, named Khangal. It is celebrated for possessing a very early and valuable copy of the Armenian Gospels. I went to the church to look for it, and found the marks of recent destruction both in the church and in the ruins in the neighbourhood. The Armenian brethren, to whom I had unfortunately no introduction, told me that the book had been carried off by the Turks. That was true, but they did not tell me, what I found out afterwards, that the whole village had performed a three days' fast, in order to save money enough to buy back their precious book from the robbers. Under such circumstances I should not have been likely to get very far in the negotiations for the transfer of the book to a place of safety, and I was obliged to leave without having seen anything of the splendid volume. As I have already intimated, there had been plunder, and I think massacre also, in the village, but this is so common a thing that one almost gives up registering it.

At Sivas one strikes the northern civilisation; and from this point on, the scenery becomes more beautiful, the vegetation richer, and the towns and villages are more and more Swiss in their appearance. Pretty tiled roofs begin to appear, ornamental balconies, and the like. Then there is a beautiful American Mission, where we had the heartiest of welcomes from Mr. and Mrs. Hubbard, and from Mr. and Mrs. Perry. There is a British Consulate, presided over by Major Bulman, and an American ditto, whose head is Dr. Jewett. The French Consulate was, I think, vacant. From all of these we received the warmest welcome, though I think Major Bulman was not quite pleased with me for going to the American Mission as headquarters, instead of wrapping myself up in the folds of his hospitable Union Jack. I may say also that I don't think he quite approved of the wisdom of my conduct in preaching on the Sunday morning in the Protestant church. But what could I do? The city had been the scene of the most terrible massacre; the pastor of the church had been killed under circumstances that in many ways reminded me of the story of Polycarp. When I tell a little of his story, it will be clear enough that it was an immense honour to me to stand in his place and speak to his people, even at the risk of some misunderstanding on the part of the Turks.

He was in the bazaar on the day of the massacre, and at the hour of noon the signal was made for the attack upon the Armenians. He fled to a khan, and being pursued, he, with other Armenians, took refuge in an upstairs room, from which there was no escape. Here they were first robbed of their valuables, and afterwards, by relay after relay of soldiers and fanatics, required to abandon their religion and exchange Christ for Mahomet. This was kept up until five in the afternoon, and then the minister declared to them openly and finally that he was not only a believer in Christ, but had been, as they knew, for many years a teacher of His Gospel, and that so he purposed to remain. They might do their worst with him, for he knew they did not mean to spare him. He raised his hands in prayer, and the controversy was ended by a bullet. "Give my salaams," said the dying man, "to Maritza" (his wife).

Now, was not this a noble piece of Christian fortitude and simplicity? It made, as they told me, a profound impression upon the Moslem population of the city. Four of the daughters of that good man were sheltered at the American Mission; the two eldest were students of Marsovan College, and preparing to be teachers. Their mother I did not see; she was absent, if I remember rightly, on an errand of mercy to some neighbouring scene of devastation. Probably this was Gurun, where 760 houses were destroyed, not one of which has up to the present been rebuilt, such is the feeling of insecurity of the population. I may add that the Turks refused the rite of burial to the martyred pastor; his body was thrown aside, along with those of the other Armenians that were with him; and of these, one that was left for dead recovered, and to him we are chiefly indebted for the account of the martyrdom.

From Sivas I reached Tokat, which is quite a beautiful little town, with excellent shops and khans. The Armenians are in the majority here, and there was no massacre. I had the opportunity, under the guidance of Miss Brewer, of the American Mission at Sivas, of visiting Henry Martyn's grave, or rather his two gravestones in the Protestant cemetery. The first of these, a flat stone, is the original monument to him, placed originally in the Armenian graveyard under the orders of Claudius Rich, the British Consul at Baghdad; the other is a more imposing stone monument erected by Dr. van Lennep, a former American missionary. The first of these monuments, a stone slab, was evidently inscribed by some one who had a copy to work from which he did not understand, for there are some curious misreadings in it. It runs as follows:—

<pre>
              REV. VIR
           GUG. MARTINO
         SACER. AC. MISS. ANGLO
         QUEM: IN. PATR. REDI.
              DOMINUS
       HIC. BERISAE. AD. SB. VOC.
        PIUM. D. EIDEL. Q. SER.
           A.D.   M.DCCCXII
          HUNC. LAP. CONSAC.
               C. I. R.
         A.D. M. (D?) CCCXII.
</pre>

I have underlined two stone-cutter's errors (*sb.* for *sc.*, and *eidel* for *fidel*). The letters C. I. R. stand for Claudius

I. Rich. Notice Rich's mistake in calling him William Martyn. Dr. van Lennep's inscription is wordy and unsatisfactory; I transcribed the English version of it. But it had one advantage. It told the date of Martyn's birth at Truro, February 18, 1781, and the date of his death at Tokat, October 16, 1812, and furnished the information that, in the thirty-one years of his short life, he had translated the Scriptures into Hindostanee and Persian.

I mention these points, not only as information, but because I am afraid I have not always done Henry Martyn sufficient justice. The fact is that I do not appreciate the school of piety which he represents, and of which he is one of the few saints; it is a morbid school, and wanting in intellectual and moral courage. However, I see clearly that Martyn's life ought to be judged by what was accomplished in its brevity, and not to be contrasted with the work or the failures of those who had a longer time than he to work or fail in. The Armenian Protestants have him in their calendar, as the saint of Tokat.

From Tokat I passed through Amasia to Marsovan, where there is the finest equipped of all the American colleges. It was vacation time, so I had no opportunity of meeting the students. Mr. and Mrs. White and Mr. Riggs received me warmly, and on the Sunday Mr. Riggs interpreted for me, while I spoke to a most interesting congregation in the Protestant church. Marsovan was very roughly handled, but seemed to have recovered. The money sent to them for relief had been largely spent in setting fifty looms going, and the sale of the pretty striped fabrics which they produce had already brought in the whole of the money expended as capital, so that they looked forward hopefully to keeping the population alive through the winter.

At Amasia, which is a large and flourishing city, I understood that the damage done had been entirely met by contributions amongst the Armenians themselves, and that they had neither asked for nor received a penny of relief money. The Armenians have in many places helped one another nobly, but this kind of charity does not get into the newspapers or subscription-lists.

Marsovan College has, *inter alia*, a fine workshop, with excellent machinery, under the charge of an Armenian from Mr. Edison's shops on the other side of the Atlantic.

You can see by these stray notes that the civilisation on the north side of the Taurus ranges is quite a different thing from that in the interior. We begin even to find Greek villages; and on the way from Marsovan to the sea there are baths with Greek and Roman inscriptions, which tell of the early development of this part of the country, and of the persistence, to some extent at least, of the ancient culture. The landscape, too, has changed, and the weather. The cloudless sky has been replaced by an overcast one in the English manner, and the clouds hang low upon the hills, and the wind had veered permanently into the north. When I first noticed this the thought flashed across my mind, "Why, this is Pontus, which Tertullian has derided in the opening of his treatise against Marcion." Yes, this was the native land of that great heretic of the second century, who denied the God of the Old Testament to be the God and Father of our Lord Jesus Christ. This is the country where "the day is never clear and the sun never cheerful, where the sky is always overcast and the whole year is wintry, and where every wind that blows is from the north;" and to this gloomy country he compares Marcion, who was born there—"Marcion, more murky than the cloud, more chill than the winter, more abrupt than the Caucasus." There is no reason to suppose Tertullian had ever visited the Pontus; his language betrays loans from some work on countries and climates. And certainly if he had come from the parched interior and the burning south winds of the desert, he would not have scolded so at clouds and the cool north breeze. So I said to myself that perhaps he might have also failed to understand Marcion, or knew him only by unjust and imperfect report. We would much like to hear Marcion speak on his own account; his message might be useful even in our day and generation.

Of the arrival at Samsoun and the passage to Constantinople and the massacre there, and the journey home, there is little need to write. As you know, I had the pleasant company of three American ladies, who had come from Van by way of Batoum; one of them is known to the whole world for her service to the suffering. Dr. Grace Kimball's two companions, Miss Frazer and Miss Huntington, have also done good work in this painful and continually extending field of suffering and sorrow.   J. R. H.

II.

Addenda on Progress of Rebuilding Villages near Harpoot.

(1.) Dr. Barnum reports (October 6) :—" You inquire about building in Hooeli (Hoo-i-loo, visited by J. R. and H. B. H.). The work is going on very successfully there, although it has been interrupted occasionally by the threats of the Turks and by fear. Permission for roofing-in the chapel has not yet been obtained, although I have given them some money for the purchase of timber, which is now very cheap."

(2.) Mr. Hallward reports (October 6) that the work of rebuilding ruined villages (in which we have a share) has been going on successfully in his district. " I buy," says he, " wood and tools for the villagers, and they do the rest. This has certainly been money well laid out. Kiabi, the village you saw, has been set on its legs again, to a limited extent, of course, but enough to give the people shelter for the winter."

III.

Further Report on the Eghin Massacre, &c.

HARPOOT, *October* 6, 1896.

Since the disaster at Eghin scarcely a person has come from there; even the regular muleteers have not come. A soldier from this city, who had a share in the massacre, has come, and he was much affected in telling his Armenian neighbours of what had taken place there, especially of the heart-rending appeals of the women. Letters received by post to-day place the number of killed at more than 2500.

The proportion of men to the women and children remaining alive is very small. The pastor writes that in his service last Sunday there were 200 women and children and only ten men. I understand that letters have been received to-day from women in Eghin begging that they might be brought here, so as to escape the insults of Turks.

The evidences multiply that there was a plan for a general mas-

P

sacre, of which the affair at Eghin was but a part, but that it was countermanded, perhaps through the influence of the Ambassadors at Constantinople. Some suppose that it has been merely postponed.

Hundreds of Armenians are arriving here who have been expelled from Constantinople. They are mostly in a very pitiable condition. They were not allowed to go to their lodgings to secure their clothing and comforts for the journey, or even to their shops to arrange their business. They were hustled away without any ceremony. The most of these men were bread-winners in Constantinople for their families here. Many of them, with their families, will now be dependent upon charity.

The Charsanjak region, to the north-east of us, is ruled and oppressed by a few feudal chiefs. They control the lands, the gardens and vineyards, and even the houses of the people. In many cases this summer, the tenants were not allowed to harvest the grain which they had sown. Their fields were given to others to reap; yet they did not venture to make complaint. Mr. Fontana, the Consul, gave to the Vali here a few of the names of the men thus despoiled, and an imposing commission was sent to investigate. The poor tenants, through fear, denied the truth. A Turk of the same district is building a large house, wholly with forced labour. This is the custom of the district, to exact labour without wages. It was one of the charges investigated with the same result as the others.

LETTER No. XXXIV.

ON THE EVE OF SETTING OUT FROM HARPOOT FOR ARABKIR AND EGHIN — THE LATE PANIC : MASSACRE AVERTED — THAT AT EGHIN CARRIED OUT BY THE CITIZENS : ALLEGED REVOLUTIONARY CAUSE FALSE — AT ARABKIR, THE PEOPLE STARVING — THE REPAIRED SCHOOLHOUSE AT HARPOOT WELL FILLED — COLLEGE DOING EXCELLENT WORK.

HARPOOT, *October* 4, 1896.

DEAR FRIENDS,—I do not like to leave you so long without a circular letter, as it is likely to be some time before I write again if I miss this post, and so will send a short letter to-night, hoping that if I am permitted to address you again from Sivas, it will be with much of interest (necessarily painful, alas!) to tell concerning Arabkir and Eghin, to which we expect to go at once.

You all know what a time of panic we passed through here a short time since. This panic extended all over this vilayet, and indeed, as we hear from letters from the missionaries in other parts, in many other places as well. No doubt another general massacre was contemplated at Harpoot, but something mercifully intervened to prevent its execution; and so in this vilayet the Damocles sword only fell on one large town, though, alas! in one or two smaller places also.

Eghin was spared last year because a large bribe was

paid to avert a massacre, but *this time* no such mercy was shown, and the ruin of the Christian population has been very complete, the first and most leading men of the community, and especially of the Protestants, being carefully sought out and killed.

This massacre was not carried out (we are informed) by the Kurds alone, as in so many places, but by the *citizens of the town* and the military. The excuse was, of course, that revolutionary spirits were inciting the people to insurrection, which, it is needless to say to you, had not one spark of truth in it from beginning to end; for the only uncertain or difficult character among the Armenians had left the town some time previously, and all remaining were perfectly quiet, law-abiding, or rather, enduring, citizens.

We are so very thankful that we have permission to go there at once and carry relief. We have been praying about it ever since we heard of the trouble, for now that the college is in working order and going on smoothly, and Mr. Gates has pretty much recovered from the fever he lately suffered from, he feels that he should visit the stricken town *without delay*, and so we all feel who are going. He has some funds, and I also have some, having heard of the safe arrival of £300 more from the Friends' Fund, and of more as on the road, and having a balance from the first £1000 which I had reserved for Van, and shall now use for Eghin and Arabkir, my way having been closed as to going to Van for the present.

We go on horseback to Arabkir first. Here Mr. Gates will make distribution of money for rebuilding the houses, giving each family £5—rather a small sum towards shelter for the winter, but enough to put up something to be added to as the people are able. There is much hunger there now, as the relief was stopped some time since, and the weaving industry, on which they depend, has not yet begun again, and although £2000 worth of material for work has now (quite lately) been promised from England, it has not yet come, and the people have fallen between these two stools, and have been and are *in a suffering condition*. I propose, therefore, to spend several hundred liras there in providing food for the present immediate and future necessity to carry them on until they shall be able to earn something for themselves. The accounts we hear are very terrible, and no doubt will soon be verified by our own eyes and ears.

We propose starting to-morrow if our guards arrive in time. If not, on Tuesday, and our party will consist, beside Miss Bush and myself, Mr. Gates, and Mr. Browne, a missionary just returned to the "Station" from America, who has had twenty years' experience of the country, and is an earnest, warm-hearted, go-ahead American, full of zeal, and not without a considerable fund of cheerfulness, and sometimes of humour as well, so we are rather a satisfactory party.

But it is time to close this hasty letter, especially as I am tired to-night, having addressed three farewell meetings, and gone through as well many personal partings with dear people to whom I have become quite attached during my long stay here, and who, I believe, love me also; and to-morrow it will not be easy to bid a long farewell to this beloved mission station, much as I have been longing for the time to arrive when I could enter once again into more active work.—So with affectionate farewells to you also, I remain yours as ever,

HELEN B. H.

P.S.—The Protestant schoolhouse in the other part of the city, which we gave £40 to repair before R. left, I saw to-day in *capital order*, and 120 children are in daily attendance! I also yesterday visited every department of this college, and the girls' schools adjoining, containing in all over 600 students, and was much impressed with the very good work being done, and the excellent order maintained. God grant that nothing may ever overturn this grand work; but rather that, obtaining the indemnity demanded, new buildings may arise from the ruins of the old, and the missionaries' plans for extending the work be fulfilled.

LETTER No. XXXV.

DEPARTURE FROM HARPOOT—DELAYS, FAREWELLS—TOILSOME JOURNEY—ARABKIR—A FINE CITY, IN RUINS — THE BETTER CLASSES IN POVERTY—VISITS FROM THE WOMEN TILL STOPPED BY THE GOVERNOR—A HEROIC TURKISH ZAPTIEH: VISIT TO HIS SICK-BED.

ARABKIR, *October* 6, 1896.

DEAR FRIENDS,—To the last moment of leaving Harpoot it seemed very doubtful whether we could get off. Our *teskerchs* had not come, nor our *zaptiehs*, and the Consul, whom we had expected in the morning, did not appear either, and so we dressed for our journey and sat down to lunch (after which we were to make our start for a five hours' ride), with rather heavy hearts.

Pretty soon it seemed as if our fears were to be realised, as a message from the Consul reached us that the Vali had requested that we would defer our visit, but that he had insisted, and hoped for the best; that, however, he had promised for us if we went that we would not enter Eghin for ten days (this, of course, to give the authorities there time to remove, as far as possible, the traces of the recent bloody work before our arrival). Later the Consul arrived, and later still, the soldiers, and then we knew we were *really to go*—but not till the very last moment!

After so long a stay at Harpoot, you can imagine that the last farewells meant a wrench for me at least, and indeed all the previous morning farewell deputations, and callers, had been coming to see me, one being a number of the leading Protestant men (the pastor included) of one of the churches, and a visit of this sort is something that cannot be hurried; and so packing has to be let take care of itself. These Oriental peoples do not feel as we do about last and first moments, but always come both to speed the parting and welcome the coming guest at the wrong time, just when English people would have the consideration to leave them in quiet; yet one cannot complain, even inwardly, they are so courteous and unconscious of being out of place.

However, all these partings over, the last words said, and handkerchiefs waved for the last time to the Mission Station, we started out—the Consul and Dr. and Mrs. Barnum accompanying us for about an hour. I will not detain you with the details of the journey, except to say that it was a pretty hard one on account of our having to keep with the mules because of carrying so much money for relief, and as they did not unload in the middle of the day we were nine hours without food one day—and kept in the saddle pretty much all day long—which was a severe tax on my newly returning strength—though our missionary friends made light of it, and Miss Bush (who is a wonderful woman) did not mind at all.

We reached this city on the third day, and received the usual warm welcome from all classes of Christians. The Protestant mission station here was not destroyed when the massacre took place, because an influential Turkish colonel lives on the adjoining premises, and is friendly to the pastor and to Christians generally; so he protected this house and others in this neighbourhood, while the ten other Christian quarters were destroyed and reduced to heaps of ruins.

This must have been a really fine city before its destruction; the houses which remain are far prettier than those of any city I have yet visited in Asia Minor, and with the lovely gardens, and glorious mountains and hills around, it must have been a most attractive spot; and here, they say, numbers of Armenian merchants, after living their business lives at Constantinople or in Egypt, &c., retired and built beautiful residences in which to spend a peaceful close of life. These houses are almost every one razed to the ground, and the merchants are either butchered or in abject poverty. One of them, seventy years of age, called on Miss B. and myself yesterday and told such a tale; and the gentlemen of our party from eight in the morning till six at night, with hardly ten minutes' intermission for lunch, are hearing the recitals of such cases one after another, with their secretary at hand making out the list for relief, according to their decision of each case's need.

Miss Bush and I commenced a similar work with the dear women, having a prepared list, and admitting them to our room one by one. In this way we had heard the sad and terrible tales of about thirty, nearly all widows, whose husbands had been killed—when the *kaimakam* (governor) stopped us. "What do these ladies want with our women? they are writing stories to send to England!" so he forbade any more coming to us.

I wish, dear friends, you could have seen these women—many of them the wives and daughters of the merchants aforesaid — ladies who lately were the mistresses of beautiful homes, some of whom had on earlier visits entertained Miss Bush most hospitably. Each entered our room with her head and face veiled; then she came, at my request (after the usual salutation), to sit by me; then at our first words of inquiry and kindly pressure of the poor hands came the invariable burst of tears; then, after soothing and encouragement, the tale of woe, the promise of help, the word of sympathy, and the closing salutation, and she retires as quietly as she entered. Often in parting, however, after kissing our hands and retiring, the dear women would come quickly back and embrace one or both of us, kiss my cheeks fervently, my hands again, and *twice, my feet* as well, lay their heads on our shoulders, salute again, burst into fresh tears, cover themselves all over with their veils, and go out weeping.

All through our two mornings thus employed, through our open windows we were nearly deafened with the drum-beating going on in the next house, because of the circumcision at one time of five of the colonel's little sons. Every hour, nearly every minute since we came, has this hideous "tom-toming," the Turkish as well as Chinese expression of rejoicing, been going on, dreary in the extreme, and a painful contrast to the weeping and lamentation in this house.

Yesterday Miss Bush went to the colonel's house to share the festivities with a large company of Turkish ladies. I was also invited but declined, my apology being that I was not very well. In the afternoon, feeling a little revived, I went with Miss Bush on quite another errand, although it *was* to visit a Turk.

Last year, a day before the massacre here, Miss Bush and another lady missionary left Arabkir to return to Harpoot, it being most important for them to rejoin the Harpoot party. They were in great danger from bands of Kurds, who thronged the whole intermediate country. With great difficulty they obtained a horse soldier as well as one on foot to accompany them. On the road the horse soldier was twice stopped by Kurds, who demanded that the ladies should be given over to them, and one Kurd said he would kill Miss Bush and have her horse; the *zaptieh* replied that he would himself be killed before they should touch the ladies, and so he carried them safely through the three days from point to point of danger. His name was —— ——, a poor soldier, worthy of much honour.

He is a native of this place and a *kaimakam's* son, though poor now, and lives about an hour's ride over the hills, and Miss Bush, having heard that he was very ill, kindly allowed me to accompany her in visiting him, which I felt very glad to be able to do, and so, attended by one of our men and a *zaptieh*, we started out, and had to begin with a most lovely ride through a succession of wonderful mountain passes, bringing us at last to a burst of Alpine scenery both exquisite and grand in the extreme, and such that, were it only accessible, would attract the entire touring world.

We paid it our tribute of admiration, and praised God

that such beauty had cheered our eyes, and then dismounting, entered a not uncomfortable nor uncleanly house, and were very kindly received by the poor wife. Soon we were permitted to enter the sick man's room and to sit on a cushion laid close by his side on the floor, and to see the best side of the Turk. He extended his hand, and Miss Bush took the poor, thin, trembling hand in hers, and spoke so tenderly to him, it did my heart good; and then she told him who I was, and as I thanked him on behalf of my country for saving her life at the risk of his own, he took my hand in both of his so gratefully. We stayed a long time with him, and both of us offered a word of prayer for him in English, and he would not let us go without refreshment, and I will tell you what the wife brought us. First, sherbet, then coffee, then a little table was brought in and placed between us, and a tray followed with *leben*, or sour curd, honey, dried cream, butter, and sweetmeats, and a sheet of their native bread. Oh, how the sick man watched that nothing should be omitted due to paying us the highest honour! It was so thoroughly the reverse side of the picture that I am accustomed to in a Turk, that it touched me very much. Then, knowing that in spite of this hospitality he was almost penniless, we both gave him a little present, which he hid under his bed, and for which he gave us outpourings of gratitude, only begging that our present *zaptieh*, a bad-looking man, might not know of our having given it.

Probably this was because if it were known, either it would be stolen or create jealousy. Indeed Miss B. says the story of his goodness to her *must not be published with his name*, or it may ruin him; but for my part I think in a very little while he will be beyond the confusions of this world and its power to injure, and in the presence of his God, where I can but believe he will be tenderly and mercifully dealt with. Oh, how he looked at us with his great dark eyes! and how tightly he held our hands in his white, delicately shaped, trembling ones, as if he could not bear for us to go! To my mind we represented to him an idea—only vaguely comprehended—of a totally different order of life and thought and love from that around him, and he had *unity of spirit with us* rather than with *it*, and tried in his poor way to express it. God bless and save him, and may we meet him again above!

With this recital I will close this letter, reserving the finish of our visit at Arabkir for my next, and then will come Eghin.—Your affectionate friend,

HELEN B. H.

LETTER No. XXXVI.

I. LETTER FROM H. B. H.—VISITING THE WOMEN AT ARABKIR; A MEETING WITH THEM—DISORDER HARSHLY QUELLED BY THE SEXTON—JOURNEY TO EGHIN: A ROMANTIC LITTLE CITY, RUINS OF BEAUTIFUL HOUSES: SAD TALES OF THE MASSACRE THERE, AND AT FIVE NEAR VILLAGES—THE BEREAVED WOMEN IN THEIR HOMES—PROVISION OF WHEAT, BEDDING, ETC., FOR WINTER NEEDS.
II. LETTER FROM MISS BUSH, EGHIN.
III. LETTER FROM MISS SHATTUCK, OURFA.

I.

Eghin, *October* 15, 1896.

DEAR FRIENDS,—As the dear Arabkir women were forbidden to come to us, Miss Bush and I adopted, during our last two days there, the other alternative, of visiting some of the most needy and worthy of them, on our list —a *zaptich* accompanying, by Government orders. He proved himself, however, a very nice friendly young man, who helps rather than hinders us. At one of these visits the gratitude of the dear woman to whom I had given help (a young widow whose husband had been killed), carried her farther than anything I have previously met with, and beyond it I do not think the expression of gratitude can go. She not only embraced me, and kissed my hands and feet, but came back weeping, and, as I reclined on the divan, lifted my "reluctant" feet, and *kissed the soles of my boots* (all dusty as they were!). I tried, of course, to prevent her when I saw her purpose, but in vain.

Our Sunday was a busy one for some of our party, and in the afternoon Miss Bush and I held a meeting for women in the Protestant church, which was crowded to overflowing — a large number, Gregorians and others, standing. While we spoke they behaved beautifully, but afterwards there was a good deal of pushing and surging of the crowd (mostly to reach us), and the soldier and sexton interfered to preserve order in true Eastern style, and I must say, of the two, the sexton was the worse! The soldier used his sheathed sword a little, not severely, but the way the sexton belaboured the women with a stick, on back and shoulder, to drive them to the door, quite took my breath away, and made Miss Bush, who was commander-in-chief both secular and ecclesiastical for the time being, *fly upon him*, and with her own good hands disengage his from a poor woman, at the same time administering a verbal reproof of no mean force, I should judge! These native Protestant Churches are wonderfully in advance of the Gregorian in every way, and the pastors are generally fairly educated men, with Geikie and Farrar in their libraries, but I shall not go so far as to endorse all the *sextons* after this!!!

We had a very early rise yesterday, the 14th, but not so early a start, owing to the slowness of our muleteers, getting off only at 7.15, and it was just ten hours later that we came in sight of Eghin, after a beautiful but very fatiguing ride up and down mountain sides and passes, and at last for two or three hours along a defile, through which flows the Euphrates, or a very large tributary thereto; on one side the mountains rise in every imaginable variety of beauty, grandeur, and sublimity, and on the other, coming down in sheer precipices to the road-side, rocks and hills of many hundred feet in height rise directly above us, overshadowing our pathway.

Eghin is itself the most surprising of romantic little cities, buried amid its surrounding mountains in a sea of verdure, which yet rises terrace upon terrace high up one mountain slope, with occasional beautiful residences peeping out above the general bower of large and most luxuriant trees of many varieties. (See Murray's "Guide to Asia Minor.") The narrow but very clean streets are all flights of steps, or stairs up and down, bordered by these leafy gardens, and as you ride up and down them you see nothing but walls—with gates where each house opens on to the so-called street—tree tops, and above them the mountain tops. This remark applies, however, alone to the uninjured parts of the city. We rode yesterday for a quarter of an hour through one district, and have since visited others, where the walls were all down, disclosing ruins of the most painful kind, all blackened by recent fire. Hundreds of once beautiful houses are now nothing but blackened ruins, still showing, however (and in this different to Arabkir, which is but heaps upon heaps), in the Christian quarters remains of their massive stone walls, numerous and spacious apartments, and beautiful woodwork—one house now in ruins is said to have contained seventy rooms. What words can depict the misery and desolation of these ruined homes lately so happy!

It is a month to-day since the massacre began, upon the wicked excuse of seditious plots in the town, of which there was not, of course, really the least trace, the only at all revolutionary Armenian having previously arrived at Harpoot from Eghin.

. . . . .

We are staying here, as we stayed at Arabkir, on the Protestant mission premises. It is a fine set of buildings, and happily spared from destruction, though thoroughly looted and all the windows gone, and the pastor's house robbed of every particle of furniture.

Saturday, 17th.—We have been here now three days, and have met many of the sufferers from the massacre, and have heard many of their sad, terrible tales; one or two of these I will recount.

The leading Protestants were, as usual, of all the Christians the most hated by the Turks, and were hunted to the death with hardly an exception,—some shot, others killed with sword and axe, and one of the noblest of all, who had eluded detection during the three days given for massacre, was killed openly by having his head crushed by heavy stones beaten against it, when he was in the street and supposed himself safe, after the massacre was over. "But you may not kill me now," he said; "orders have come to stop the killing." "We may no longer kill with guns," was the reply, "but stones are different, and we may use them;" so he died.

One Protestant (a very intimate friend of the Harpoot missionaries, especially so of Mr. Browne, who mourns his loss almost as that of a brother), and a graduate of Harpoot College, was very rich and influential, as well as eminently good and useful to the town. He had in consequence long been an object of jealousy to some leading Turks, and was named to Mr. Gates, by the *kaimakam*, as the head of the (imaginary) revolutionary committee. When the *kaimakam* said this, it was very hard for our missionary friends not to deny it indignantly, knowing him to have ever been most loyal to the Government, and most opposed to any but constitutional methods of reform. (However, from prudential reasons they held their peace.) He was *killed most cruelly*,—first shot, then cut with swords and knives, and afterwards (some say while still living, others, when the breath had just left him, and who knows which is true?) a stake was driven down his throat with the savage sneer, "Here is your Beyship!"—a Beyship, or Lordship, being supposed to have been one object of his ambition. Those killed mostly had their throats cut, or were killed with axes, 100 of which had been made by order of the City Council.

. . . . . .

One commentary on this rebellion, so "*bravely*" quelled by the Turks, is that not one single shot was fired by an Armenian, or a Turk killed. On the other hand a million liras' (or Turkish pounds) worth of property was destroyed or stolen (for this was the richest of Armenian cities though so small), of which, it is said, £20,000 have found their way into four Turkish pockets, the heads of the Turkish community here. For the accuracy of these figures I do not vouch, but —— brought the information to our dinner-table to-night.

Five neighbouring villages were attacked at the same time as Eghin, and many were killed. At one of these, Pingyan, a number of women (fifteen) and girls threw themselves into the Euphrates and were drowned. Miss Bush and I have been out paying visits to the poor women in their homes here as at Arabkir, and these visits have been very much the same as those, though these women are of a higher social grade as a rule, comparable to our middle class at home. They receive us always in their despoiled homes with an outburst of tears, and generally Miss Bush is embraced as an old friend would be anywhere after such a calamity, and sometimes I am also. Then we sit down in what remains of the "seat of honour," and they salaam us with great ceremony as if greeting us for the first time; others come in and do the same, and every one salutes every one else, and this takes a deal of time. Then, seated around us, they very soon give full play to their grief and anguish, and various terrible recitals follow each other in quick succession, emphasised by Oriental gesticulation. Then comes the weeping and wailing of many together, and then *we put in our words*, or Miss Bush does, exhorting to faith, patience, and hope, and then we close with Bible reading and prayer.

Many of these women have lost their husbands, and all, husband or sons, father or brother, mostly killed before their eyes. One dear woman, at whose house we were, had had her husband and two sons of 18 and 20 years of age killed. One woman had had two dear boys killed, and a kindly soldier who knew that their dead bodies were lying right in her path as she was coming down the street, called to her with real humanity: "Don't come down that way!" she was just turning aside when another brutally called to her, "Yes, come; I have something to show you here;" and so she went. "Do you know them?" he said. "Yes!" she replied. "If you who slew them know them, should not I who bore them?" This she told us herself, poor creature. But I must not go any further into the details of this tragedy, or I shall only sicken you, when I would interest.

We have the great comfort, amid the gloom, of knowing that we are here with help in our hands, and that we hope to leave the town prepared in some measure to face the winter, the cold of which is already commencing. From the Friends' Fund I have calculated that I can spend about £1500 here, and we are planning how to use it to the best account. Wheat is cheap now, and probably a good deal will go in that, and every needy family will have enough given them to carry them through the winter. The next need is bedding, for the Kurds and other depredators always relieve every household of these necessaries, then clothing and firing; then I propose putting in the glass to the windows of the mission premises (all broken), to make it at once usable, and to do other things of the kind. I hear also that, while most of the Christian families have had their Bibles destroyed, there is both here and at Arabkir a large stock on hand for sale, and the pastor petitions us to buy and distribute those to the families who have none, which I shall probably do.

We shall in these various ways find plenty to do for another week, which will probably be about the length of the remainder of our visit, and then our little party will separate, Mr. Browne escorting me towards Sivas, and the others returning to Arabkir and Harpoot.—With love, I remain, yours truly,

HELEN B. H.

Oct. 31.—Arrived safely at Sivas. I could not post at Arabkir or Egbin.

II.

Extracts from a Letter from Miss Bush, also from Eghin.

October 24, 1896.

Everybody is in a rush of work this morning; a carpenter is in my room, putting in windows, by the kindness of Mrs. H., so that after this Harriet and I will not have to close the shutters on cold days and live in the dark, or shiver in the cold with them open. She also had the windows of the chapel all put in, as they were completely ruined by the Kurds.

Yesterday morning Mr. Gates commenced to give relief money, having been occupied every day previous with the making out of lists.

There have been daily morning prayer-meetings this week, but yesterday, when we saw that the men could not come, and also this morning, we turned it into a women's meeting and had a great crowd. Mrs. H. speaks to the women, and of course I translate, and speak some myself after she finishes. Yesterday morning she spoke on forgiving our enemies. This morning occurred a remarkable coincidence. Just before our half-past six breakfast, I became fascinated with the 49th chapter of Isaiah. As I read the verse I love, "Yea, they may forget, yet I will not forget thee," the prayer rose in my heart, "Lord, grant that Mrs. H. may choose this to speak on this morning." We saw that the Protestant brethren had not come, so Mrs. H. and I started, and she said, opening her little daily text-book, "I wish to speak on this, 'Yea, they may forget, yet I will not forget thee!'" The Spirit was surely with us, for many women wept, and the closest attention was given while we spoke, and many afterwards crowded about us to kiss our hands and give us thanks. It was a touching sight.

Mrs. H. and I have done a little calling this week and seen many women. We had meetings with the women Sunday, Monday, and Wednesday, with very large attendances. I have felt as I went about, as if I was in an awful dream, and was almost stupefied with the sorrow of it all.

Mr. Gates looked pretty weary last evening, after his first day of distribution. The people are so importunate, poor, wretched, and sorrowful, yet they seem much comforted by our coming, and we are glad to have reached them so soon.

III.

Extracts from a Letter from Miss Shattuck to H. B. H.

OURFA, *September* 28, 1896.

Would you could see, as I saw last Friday on going my round, the quiet orderly schools *without exception*, the pupils studious and advancing rapidly, where at the beginning of our co-operative school work was but the old Gregorian system of studying aloud and general confusion. I could almost weep for joy at the blessing of God upon my honest though feeble efforts, and I know of your constant prayers. They will never want to slip back if this can be kept up through the entire year, and they really taste the better way.

I am so thankful for the gift of money for wheat for our needy families. Such happy grateful creatures would surely give joy to the angels in heaven. It is a great help, and I feel less anxious for them otherwise, now the "staff of life" is provided.

October 10, 1896.

The last mail brought a long-expected letter from Dr. Lepsius. He authorises our taking in fifty more orphan children immediately, making his number one hundred in all.

Do you know that your good country-people have generously responded to Miss Mellinger's appeal, and sent us enough to supply the needy with *bourgoul*[1] till spring! We praise God for this special relief of distress we saw

---

[1] A preparation of wheat.

ahead. Over 700 families have received their portions, and before the rains are getting it cooked and dried. It is *so good!*

Schools are in excellent state. Teachers and pupils full of enthusiasm; 1265 pupils enrolled. I wish you might go the rounds of visitation in the fifteen rooms and meet our eighteen teachers.

You see God used you for a *great blessing* to Ourfa, and we all praise Him for it. I wish to tell of our eighteen Bible-women and their work, but I am unable for want of time.

LETTER No. XXXVII.

JOURNEY FROM SIVAS TO MARSOVAN VIÂ TOKAT—HARD TRAVEL—WELCOME AT MARSOVAN—AN IDEAL MISSION THERE—TOILSOME JOURNEY TO SAMSOUN—LETTER FROM HARPOOT, STATING PRESENT DIFFICULTIES AND THE APPARENT INTENTION OF THE GOVERNMENT TO CLOSE THE MISSION SCHOOLS, ETC.—RELIEF WORK IN EGHIN.

MARSOVAN, *November* 18, 1896.

DEAR FRIENDS,—After a very full Sunday at Sivas, with one very crowded meeting of men and women together in the church, and two Bible-classes, besides the little evening service with the dear missionary band, and a very secular Monday, full of innumerable last things, and preparations for our five days' journey, we set out on the tenth from the shadow of Christian civilisation into our "wilderness journey" once again.

But I was more highly favoured than I had expected, for instead of having only servants and *zaptiehs* as my companions, as had seemed likely, on the last day one of the lady missionaries who very much needed a change, Mrs. Perry by name, decided to pay a visit to Marsovan, and to take the opportunity of accompanying me, being protected in her turn by a Circassian *cavass* belonging to the American Consulate, armed with ornamental dirk, dagger, and pistol, and presenting an imposing appearance.

I had an *onbashee* (or officer over ten men) and a common *zaptieh* to take care of me, and they came all the way with us to Marsovan—a most unusual proceeding—and when they left, they carried away two good Turkish Bibles, which they seemed delighted to accept as souvenirs of our journey, and commenced reading them at once.

On our way out of Sivas we passed some very ancient archæological remains—an old gateway of great beauty and interest, and later the sheet of water where the celebrated forty martyrs were frozen to death in ancient times. The road to Tokat is very mountainous, and the tableland itself, from which the mountains rise, is from 4000 to 5000 feet above the sea-level, so you may fancy how cold it is to travel over.

At Tokat we visited the tomb of Henry Martyn, now in the Protestant mission grounds. It cost some effort to do this, as we did not reach the town till the sun had set, and then it was quite a little walk. However, by the fading light I deciphered the inscription to the memory of this pioneer of the faith, thanking God that "such as he had lived and died." We brought the native Protestant pastor back to our khan with us and gave him the best dinner, humble as it was, that I expect he had had for some time (I do not wish to be boastful, but as I made the toast and scrambled the eggs myself, I enjoyed his appreciation of them very especially, he being just then rather overworked and unable for native food).

Three days out of our five of travel we were twelve and thirteen hours on the road, and as it was considered much safer to be out in the dark early rather than late, we started two or three hours before daybreak, rising by 2 A.M. One night our men were so anxious to be in time, they had the oatmeal and hot milk for coffee ready at 12.30, and routed poor Mrs. Perry up at that hour. We each of us had our own *araba* or waggon to travel in, and when once started I wrapped up and took another nap, that is, when the bitter, bitter cold permitted, which was by no means always. My dear horse came with us, and both Mrs. Perry and I rode him for many hours each day, and so varied the mode of travel; and to Mrs. Perry I have now sold him, and have the pleasure of thinking that he will remain in the Lord's work and in loving hands, and I hope in time he may become quite "a changed character," though indeed, when "on the road" and in full work, no one could wish for a better or gentler horse.

Our last day's journey was marked by a very special mercy. It had rained heavily the day and night previously, and the roads were difficult in consequence. We, however, proceeded across the plain by a usual short cut, and had just got through some bad mud-holes, when a young man from Marsovan on his way to Amasia met us, and said we could proceed no further on that road without being mired; so he kindly led us some distance across country, to the long but passable road which finally brought us to our journey's end two hours late; and you may think how grateful we were that he met us where he did, and prevented we know not how much trouble.

About an hour from Marsovan nearly all the missionary station met us, two gentlemen and one lady on horseback, and a carriage full besides. These dear missionary people know how to give a good and beautiful welcome to weary travellers, I assure you, and I had the joy of being welcomed, not only as such by these kind friends, but specially for my husband's sake, by those who were here when he passed through.

Marsovan is a beautifully situated town, at the foot of a range of mountains, now all covered with snow, while the trees around it are still green. The college premises are the finest we have visited in this country, quite equal, I think, to Robert College itself. There is a large staff of missionaries here, and a fine efficient staff of native professors as well, who can converse fluently in English. All of them came together to call on me yesterday, and we had a very interesting time, and I found the Greek professor had been in Athens the time R. and I were there, and knew Mr. Kalopithakes, Professor Morkos, and other friends; and others had travelled in Europe and America.

The Protestant Church also sent a deputation to call on me, of seven or eight brethren, equally friendly, but all so anxious for good news, and assurances from me for their people. Oh! if only I had had the power to give them!

Here as elsewhere there are tales of distress and heroism of massacre days to hear, and much prospective suffering this winter for want of food, to try to alleviate. I am leaving my "last penny" here, metaphorically speaking, and shall send some more from Constantinople, as also to Sivas, if I find any awaiting me there.

I have heard of some very beautiful incidents here, of heroism and Christian fortitude and faith, which I shall save up to tell you when I return (as they would be quite too long to write).

On Sunday the 15th—anniversary of the massacre—I had a meeting with the 120 dear bright girls of the Girls' College, who, under their most kind and efficient teachers, Miss Gage and Miss Willard, are a credit to the Mission; and to-day, Wednesday, I am to have a women's meeting in the church, and to-morrow we leave, Mr. Riggs kindly escorting me in their spring waggon to Samsoun, as I leave my horse " Mardin " behind.

SAMSOUN, *Sunday, November* 22.

The beautiful visit at Marsovan will ever live in my memory as one of the pleasantest of my life, and was all too short and crowded. It is quite an ideal mission, with " fathers and mothers in Israel," and the young and gifted laying every power on the altar, and all the work is so divinely natural and cheerful, that it seems wonderful how such life and light can exist amid the surrounding darkness. I left most reluctantly as far as the mission station was concerned, though you know I would not delay in my home-coming a single hour that does not seem necessary from some point of view.

In spite of warm wraps and the spring waggon in which Mr. Riggs so kindly drove me to the coast (a three days' journey of two short and one long day), the journey, between the cold and the jolting and the almost sleepless nights, was about all I could stand, and I counted every minute almost on the last day, thanking my heavenly Father with a very grateful heart *that it was* the last day, for I felt as if another would be impossible (doubtless an exaggerated impression); but oh! how glad I was no words can express, to see the red tiles and white houses of Samsoun, and the black Black Sea, literally so from clouds, stretching out before me.

To-day it is beautifully sunny and fine, like an English spring day, and in the pastor's garden here—we visited them after the service—his wife has just picked me a posy with geranium and honeysuckle and carnation, which is on the table before me as I write. It is a very different climate from that of the mountainous region we have left behind us, and a very pleasant change.

I am hoping to get off to-morrow, but am not sure, and a number of "Ourfans" bound for Brusa—from Harpoot—will, I expect, travel with me (besides some others). I may send you another line from Constantinople if I find anything special to tell, but I feel very near the end of our rather one-sided correspondence now, and I do thank you much, dear friends, for all your loving interest in and patience with, my rather prosy letters.

And so with love to all, and praying for a blessing on our meeting one another again face to face if God permit,—I remain, your affectionate friend,

HELEN B. H.

Printed by BALLANTYNE, HANSON & CO.
Edinburgh and London.

SELECT LIST OF BOOKS
DEVOTIONAL AND PRACTICAL
PUBLISHED BY
JAMES NISBET & CO., LIMITED.

THE CHRISTIAN UNDER REVIEW.
A SERIES OF WORKS ON PRACTICAL CHRISTIAN LIFE.
Small crown 8vo.

THE CHRISTIAN'S INFLUENCE. By the Ven. WILLIAM MACDONALD SINCLAIR, D.D., Archdeacon of London. 2s.

THE CHRISTIAN'S START. By the Very Rev. the DEAN OF NORWICH. 1s.

THE MORAL CULTURE OF THE CHRISTIAN. By the Rev. JAMES McCANN, D.D. 1s.

THE PATHWAY OF VICTORY. By the Rev. ROBERT B. GIRDLESTONE, M.A., Hon. Canon of Christ Church, and late Principal of Wycliffe Hall, Oxford. 1s.

THE CHRISTIAN'S RECREATIONS. By the Rev. HENRY SUTTON, M.A., Vicar of Holy Trinity, Bordesley. 1s.

THE CHRISTIAN'S PROGRESS. By the Ven. G. R. WYNNE, D.D., Archdeacon of Aghadoe. 1s.

THE CHRISTIAN'S DUTIES AND RESPONSIBILITIES. By the Very Rev. the DEAN OF NORWICH. 1s.

THE CHRISTIAN'S AIMS. By the Rev. ALFRED PEARSON, M.A., Incumbent of St. Margaret's Church, Brighton. 1s.

THE INTELLECTUAL CULTURE OF THE CHRISTIAN. By the Rev. JAMES McCANN, D.D. 1s.

THE CHRISTIAN'S PRIVILEGES. By the Rev. W. J. DEANE, M.A. 1s.

THE CHRISTIAN'S INHERITANCE. By the Rev. C. A. GOODHART, M.A., Incumbent of St. Barnabas', Highfield, Sheffield. 1s.

"Simple and forcible as these books are in their teaching, and brief in extent, they deserve the attention of those who direct the religious teaching of the young."—*Scotsman.*

"We dipped into these pages alike with pleasure and profit. The writers, each on his own theme, seem steadfastly to keep in view scriptural teaching, sound doctrine, and the trials and temptations which beset the daily life and walk of the believer."—*Word and Work.*

"How completely they cover the field of Christian needs is sufficiently indicated by their titles. They are well fitted to stimulate the piety and clear the views of those holding the doctrines of the Church of England."—*Liverpool Mercury.*

Works Devotional and Practical

By the Rev. H. W. WEBB-PEPLOE,
PREBENDARY OF ST. PAUL'S CATHEDRAL.

THE LIFE OF PRIVILEGE. With Portrait. Extra crown 8vo, 3s. 6d.

THE VICTORIOUS LIFE. Extra crown 8vo, 3s. 6d.

By Dean FARRAR, Dr. HORTON, Dr. CLIFFORD, Rev. E. A. STUART, &c. &c.

BIBLICAL CHARACTER SKETCHES. Crown 8vo, 3s. 6d.

By the Rev. F. BOURDILLON, M.A.,
Author of "Alone with God," "A Help to Family Worship," &c. &c.

THE PRODIGAL AT HOME AGAIN. Extra pott 8vo, cloth, 1s.

SPIRITUAL STEPPING STONES; or, The Soul's Progress, as taught in Romans v. 1-11. Extra pott 8vo, 1s.

By the Rev. E. J. HARDY,
Author of "How to be Happy though Married," "Uncle John's Talks with his Nephews," &c.

IN THE FOOTPRINTS OF ST. PAUL. Illustrated. Small crown 8vo, 2s. 6d.

By CHARLOTTE MURRAY.

MORNING SUNLIGHT. Daily Devotional Readings for One Year. Printed on specially light paper for the convenience of invalids. Extra crown 8vo, red edges, 3s. 6d.

EON THE GOOD. With Portrait. Crown 8vo, 2s. 6d.

By Rev. S. F. HARRIS,
VICAR OF WALTON-LE-DALE.

EARNEST YOUNG HEROES. Ion Keith Falconer, Hedley Vicars, Lieutenant Boldero, R.N., and Mackay of Uganda. With Portraits. Crown 8vo, 2s.

By JAAKOFF PRELOOKER,
Author of "The Hidden Jewel."

UNDER THE CZAR AND QUEEN VICTORIA. The Struggles of a Russian Reformer. Profusely Illustrated. Pott 4to, 6s.

By the Rev. W. B. BIRTT.

LIVING SACRIFICES. With Introduction by Rev. J. OSSIAN DAVIES. Crown 8vo, 1s. 6d.

Published by James Nisbet & Co., Limited.

By the Very Rev. Dean FARRAR, Principal MOULE, Bishop BARRY, &c.

Edited by the DEAN OF NORWICH.

LECTURES ON ECCLESIASTICAL HISTORY. Extra crown 8vo, 7s. 6d.

By the Rev. ANDREW MURRAY.

OUT OF HIS FULNESS. A Series of Addresses. Small Crown 8vo, 1s. 6d.

WAITING ON GOD. Extra pott 8vo, 1s.; roan, gilt edges, 2s.

THE POWER OF THE SPIRIT. With Additional Extracts from the Writings of William Law. Crown 8vo, 2s. 6d.

ABIDE IN CHRIST. New and Cheaper Edition. Small crown 8vo, 1s. net; in superior binding, 2s. 6d.

By the Rev. GEORGE EVERARD, M.A.,

Author of "Strong and Free," &c. &c.

SALVATION AND SERVICE. Extra crown 8vo, 3s. 6d.

By F. A. ATKINS,

Author of "Moral Muscle," &c. &c., and Editor of the *Young Man*.

ASPIRATION AND ACHIEVEMENT: A Book for Young Men. Cloth, small crown 8vo, 1s.

By the Rev. J. R. MILLER, D.D.,

Author of "Making the Most of Life," &c.

GLIMPSES THROUGH LIFE'S WINDOWS: Selections from the Writings of the Rev. J. R. MILLER, D.D. Small crown 8vo, with Portrait, gilt top, 2s. 6d.

GIRLS: FAULTS AND IDEALS. A Friendly Talk, with Quotations from Young Men's Letters. Crown 8vo, 6d.

YOUNG MEN: FAULTS AND IDEALS. A Friendly Talk, with Quotations from Girls' Letters. Crown 8vo, 6d.

These two booklets bound together in cloth, 1s.

By Mrs. FRANCES BEVAN.

MATELDA AND THE CLOISTER OF HELLFDE. Translations from the Book of Matilda of Magdeburg (supposed to be Dante's Matilda). Crown 8vo, 2s. 6d.

By Rev. J. BROWNLIE and Rev. Dr. M'CRIE.

HYMNS OF THE EARLY CHURCH. Translations from the Poetry of the Latin Church. Extra pott 8vo, buckram, 2s. 6d.

By the Rev. J. REID HOWATT.

THE CHILDREN'S PREACHER. A Year's Addresses and Parables for the Young. Extra crown 8vo, 6s.

A NIGHT IN BETHLEHEM FIFTY YEARS AFTER. Freely Rendered. Long fcap. 8vo, 1s. sewn ; 1s. 6d. cloth.

THE CHILDREN'S PEW. Sermons to Children. Extra crown 8vo, 6s.

THE CHILDREN'S PULPIT. A Year's Sermons and Parables for the Young. Second Edition. Extra crown 8vo, 6s.

THE CHILDREN'S ANGEL. Being a Volume of Sermons to Children. Crown 8vo, 2s. 6d.

FAITH'S STRONG FOUNDATIONS. Small crown 8vo, 1s.

YOUTH'S IDEALS. Small crown 8vo, 1s.
"So bright and cheerful, so clever and well written, yet so full of deep Christian earnestness, that we would like to see it circulated by tens of thousands."—*The New Age.*

AFTER HOURS ; or, The Religion of Our Leisure Time. With Appendix on How to Form a Library for Twenty Shillings. Small crown 8vo, 1s.

AGNOSTIC FALLACIES. Crown 8vo, 1s.
" Mr. Howatt has succeeded remarkably well in the five lectures before us. They are plain, straightforward, logical, and eminently to the point."—*Literary Churchman.*

THE CHILDREN'S PRAYER BOOK : Devotions for the Use of the Young for One Month. Cloth extra, pott 8vo, 1s.

LIFE WITH A PURPOSE. A Book for Girls and Young Men. Crown 8vo, 1s.

By Miss NUGENT.

THE PRINCE IN THE MIDST. ["Jesus our Centre. Extra pott 8vo, 1s.

By R. A. TORREY,

SUPERINTENDENT OF MR. MOODY'S BIBLE INSTITUTE, CHICAGO.

HOW TO BRING MEN TO CHRIST. Crown 8vo, 1s. 6d.

HOW TO STUDY THE BIBLE FOR GREATEST PROFIT. Crown 8vo, 1s. 6d.

THE BAPTISM WITH THE HOLY SPIRIT. Crown 8vo, 1s.

THE VEST POCKET COMPANION FOR CHRISTIAN WORKERS. In Leatherette, 1s.

Published by James Nisbet & Co., Limited.

By the Rev. J. R. MILLER, D.D.,
Author of "Making the Most of Life," &c. &c.

GLIMPSES THROUGH LIFE'S WINDOW. Small crown 8vo, with Portrait. Gilt top, 2s. 6d.

GIRLS: FAULTS AND IDEALS. With Quotations from Girls' Letters. Crown 8vo, 6d.

YOUNG MEN: FAULTS AND IDEALS. With Quotations from Young Men's Letters. Crown 8vo, 6d.

By MATTHEW HENRY.

EXPOSITION OF THE OLD AND NEW TESTAMENTS. **£2 2 0** With Practical Remarks and Observations— **and**
 In Nine Volumes. Imp. 8vo, £2, 2s. *Net*. **£1 11 6**
 In Six Volumes. Medium 8vo, £1, 11s. 6d. *Net*. **per Set**

By HARRIET E. COLVILE.

THE WAY SHE TROD. A STUDY. Small crown 8vo, 2s. 6d.

"'The Way She Trod' is a study of the development of religious sentiment and belief in a girl's character."—*Scotsman*.

FLOWER VOICES. With Illustrations. Demy 16mo, 1s.

WAFTED SEEDS. With Illustrations. Demy 16mo, 1s.

By Rev. JOSEPH PARKER, D.D.,

WELL BEGUN. A Book for Young Men. Crown 8vo, 5s.

NONE LIKE IT. A Plea for the Old Sword. Crown 8vo, 5s.

TO-DAY'S CHRIST. Long fcap., 1s. *Net*.

LIST OF BOOKS OF FAMILY PRAYERS.

By the Rev. F. B. MEYER, B.A.

PRAYERS FOR HEART AND HOME. Morning and Evening Devotions for One Month for Family and Private Use. Pott 4to, 2s. 6d.

By the Right Rev. the LORD BISHOP OF RIPON.

CHURCHMAN'S BOOK OF FAMILY PRAYERS. Printed in Red and Black. Cloth plain, pott 4to, 3s. 6d. Cloth gilt, burnished red edges, 5s.

By the Rev. J. REID HOWATT.

THE CHILDREN'S PRAYER BOOK. Being Prayers for the Use of the Young for One Month. Extra pott 8vo, 1s.

By the Rev. GORDON CALTHROP, M.A.

FAMILY PRAYERS FOR FOUR WEEKS. Imperial 16mo, 2s. 6d.

By the Rev. J. OSWALD DYKES, D.D.

DAILY PRAYERS FOR THE HOUSEHOLD FOR A MONTH. Crown 8vo, 3s. 6d.

By the Rev. GEORGE EVERARD, M.A.

BEFORE HIS FOOTSTOOL. Family Prayers for one Month. With Prayers for Special Occasions, and Introduction. Ninth Thousand. Crown 8vo, 3s.

By the Rev. J. R. MACDUFF, D.D.

MORNING FAMILY PRAYERS. Small 4to, 6s. 6d.

FAMILY PRAYERS. Small crown 8vo, 3s. 6d.

By M. L. M. DAWSON.

FAMILY PRAYERS FOR A MONTH. Demy 8vo, 1s. 6d.

DAILY PRAYERS FOR BUSY HOMES. 16mo, 6d.

LONDON: JAMES NISBET & CO., LIMITED,
21 BERNERS STREET, W.

www.ingramcontent.com/pod-product-compliance
Lightning Source LLC
Chambersburg PA
CBHW031944230426
43672CB00010B/2045